SENT FROM GOD

SENT FROM GOD

The Enduring Power and Mystery of Preaching

David H. C. Read

ABINGDON PRESS

Nashville   New York

Library of Congress Cataloging in Publication Data

READ, DAVID HAXTON CARSWELL.
  Sent from God
  1. Preaching. I. Title.
        BV4211.2.R36   251   73-18241

ISBN 0-687-37466-9

Scripture quotations noted NEB are from The New
English Bible. © the Delegates of the Oxford University
Press and the Syndics of the Cambridge University
Press, 1961, 1970. Reprinted by permission.

Scripture quotations noted Phillips are from The New
Testament in Modern English, copyright 1958 by J. B.
Phillips.

The lines (p. 17) from "O God of Earth and Altar" by
G. K. Chesterton are from *The English Hymnal,* copyright © Oxford University Press, and are reprinted by
permission.

MANUFACTURED BY THE PARTHENON PRESS AT
NASHVILLE, TENNESSEE, UNITED STATES OF AMERICA

To:

My congregations in
Coldstream, Scotland (1936–39);
P.O.W. Camps, Germany (1940–45);
Greenbank, Edinburgh (1945–49);
Edinburgh University (1949–56);
Madison Avenue Presbyterian Church,
New York City (1956 . . .)

with much gratitude and affection.

Preface

This is a book about preaching by one for whom preaching is an endless adventure. It is addressed to everyone who has an interest in the subject, and not only to preachers and seminarians.

The author is not a Jeremiah in the popular sense, but shares the real Jeremiah's feelings for the compulsion and mystery of the declaration of the Word of God. He believes in the enduring power of that Word and in the sacramental nature of true preaching. He has tried to express what that means to us today, and he hopes that he has done so without resorting to either the technical vocabulary of the theologian or the jargon of the sixties.

No one can possibly lay down the law about how sermons should be prepared and delivered. Each one "sent from God" to attempt this task has special gifts, interests, and failings. So this must be a personal statement, the sharing of one man's thoughts and hopes, in the belief that from a lively interchange new light may dawn. We need it; and the Spirit may well be about to give it in unexpected ways.

The core of this book consists of the Lyman Beecher Lectures for the year 1973. I am humbly grateful for the invitation to share in this series that is now over a hundred years old, and particularly happy to follow my predecessors in this pulpit—Henry Sloane Coffin, who delivered the lectures in 1917, and George Arthur Buttrick, who gave them in 1931.

It was a pleasure to be a guest of the Yale Divinity School, and I want to thank the faculty and students for their warm hospitality, and for the stimulating and enthusiastic audience that made lecturing there a memorable experience. I am indebted to a host of people in my attempts to think through the meaning of preaching today. My theological debts will be obvious, and I would like to thank four friends who have shared their thoughts on this topic with me—Frederick Buechner, Avery Dulles, Andrew Hamza, and Dietrich Ritschl. My gratitude also goes to Carolyn Mathis, who labored skillfully on the manuscript.

Madison Avenue Presbyterian Church
New York City, 1973

Contents

1

The Survival of the Sermon in an Age of Distraction

"How shall they preach without a hearer?"

If the title of this first chapter has a slightly defensive ring, this does not indicate that what follows will be an attempt by a preacher to justify his existence or to breathe a little life into an institution around whose body our prophets of doom are already conducting an enthusiastic wake. In the hint that was given me when I accepted the invitation to deliver the Lyman Beecher Lectures, I detected an echo of those funeral rites, for it was suggested that it is not now obligatory for the lecturer to address himself to the subject of preaching. For the last twenty years or so, we have suffered from a kind of Protestant paralysis in the very area that the great reformers viewed as central to the life of the Church. There has been a loss of nerve, a creeping sense of futility, a desire to seek new life in other directions. My decision to tackle the subject was not

11

prompted by a belief that I had something brilliant or innovative to say, but by the conviction that preaching remains an enduring mystery in the Christian Church and is as central to her life as the sacraments or social activity. Therefore, in each generation fresh thought must be given to its form, style, and peculiar place in the life and worship of the Christian community.

Since everything in the Church today from a prayer cell to a protest meeting has to be called a "celebration," let me celebrate preaching. To paraphrase Winston Churchill, I did not feel that I was summoned to deliver the Lyman Beecher Lectures in order to preside over the liquidation of the homiletic art. On the contrary, I approach this theme with a genuine conviction that we may be on the verge of a renaissance of preaching, and I detect signs already that the next seminary generation will be gripped again by the perennial excitement of the living pulpit. What follows, however, is by no means exclusively addressed to preachers or those in training. Preaching is an activity of the whole Church, and there is an urgent need for a fresh understanding of its nature by those who listen, as well as those who speak. Not nearly enough has been said on this subject in the flow of how-to books in past years. Preaching as an integral part of the total life of the Church needs to be understood by all her members, and the live participation of a congregation in the spoken Word is a neglected theme. It is worth noting, by the way, that the current disparagement of the sermon is almost exclusively a clerical phenomenon. Any poll will reveal that the laity still rank preaching ability very high among the

12

qualities desired in a pastor, and (more important) continue to have great expectations. It is my contention that they are not just indulging in nostalgic yearnings for a pattern of church life that belongs to another age, but showing a sounder theological judgment than that of most academic theorizers or the more cynical of the clergy.

There are, of course, factors in our situation today that have led to a downgrading of preaching in the popular mind during the last fifty or a hundred years. But before considering these we might remember that the sermon has always been fair game for the satirist, the humorist, and the cynic, ever since Luke described the episode of the young man who fell asleep during one of Paul's sermons. (His name was Eutychus, whence I derive the heresy of "Eutychianism" which has been with us ever since.) My dictionary has two definitions of preaching. The first is "to pronounce a public discourse on sacred subjects," which sounds both pompous and dull. The second, which is worse, is "to give advice in an offensive or obtrusive manner." The pages of the *New Yorker* and of *Punch* drew steadily on the preacher for material until he was mercifully replaced by the psychiatrist. Sydney Smith described an opponent as one who "deserves to be preached to death by wild curates," and other literary references to the sermon, from Chaucer to Mailer, are rarely complimentary. You will have noticed that the most damning thing that can be said about an aspirant for high political office is that he preaches.

All this, of course, can be interpreted as a backhanded admission of the importance of preaching, and it may be that a slackening of the satire is as unwelcome a sign to the Church as the cessation of ugly caricatures is to the politician. The point is that there is, and always has been, a popular misunderstanding of the nature of preaching, fostered by the follies of us preachers in every generation. You can hardly expect a dictionary to be theologically sensitive, but the definition of "pronouncing a public discourse on sacred subjects" is not one I propose to follow.

In a Christian context, preaching is a unique event in which human words, ordinary contemporary words, are used to declare the Word of God, the gospel of Christ as it is found in the Bible. Karl Barth's image of the preacher as the man with the Bible in one hand and the daily newspaper in the other shows what this means. Preaching is an encounter of modern man with the Word of God. It is a sacramental mystery in which, through the power of the Holy Spirit, the "bread and wine" of the everyday speech of very ordinary mortals become the vehicles for the Real Presence of Christ. The mystery has been present and central in the life of the Church since the day of Pentecost, and will be till the day of the Church Triumphant. (Perhaps the writer of the Revelation was thinking of this when he wrote that "there was silence in heaven about the space of half an hour.") Preaching is thus not an optional activity in the Church, nor is it the equivalent of a lecture or commentary. It is a sacramental act rooted in the Scriptures and experience of the Church, that has taken as many forms in different ages as the Lord's Supper, but cannot be eliminated from the living community of the Spirit. It is worth noting that Barth himself declared that the whole enterprise of his immense *Dogmatics* was founded on the belief that theology is nothing else but an attempt to understand what happens when we preach.

What we have to reckon with, then, is the contemporary climate and its effect on the practice of preaching. What is it that has led to a paralysis in some sections of Protestantism today, a loss of nerve, a discouragement, even a cynicism?

The most obvious factor among the major denominations in this country and in Europe is the decline in the number of listeners. Lecturers on preaching find it difficult to avoid finding the rationale of the sermon in the words of Paul: "Whosoever shall call upon the name of the Lord shall be saved. How then shall they call on him in whom they have not believed? and how shall they believe in him of whom they have not heard? and how shall they hear without a preacher?" It was a discouraged preacher friend who recently said ruefully in my hearing that Paul ought to have written, "How shall they preach without a hearer?" It is easy to maintain a high and hopeful concept of preaching when one envisions pews packed with an expectant congregation: it is very different when the prospect is of a tired group of twenty or thirty scattered around a sanctuary that holds a thousand. Dr. Colin Morris, writing of the English situation recently in the London *Times,* says, "All the activities of a shrinking Church tend to contract proportionately to the attention devoted to them. Empty pews . . . are not conducive to powerful preaching. This argument can, of course, be stood on its head by claiming that congregations would not be shrinking if the quality of preaching were better. The weight of the evidence does not, however, support this view. Some of the most gifted preachers of our day are unable to maintain, let alone increase their congregations."

Before we ask what may have led to the decline in the public response to preaching, we have to guard against the parochialism of this point of view. While congregations have shrunk dramatically in parts of Europe like Scandinavia, very considerably in Britain, and noticeably in the major denominations of this country, the picture is totally different in Africa, Indonesia, parts of South America, and among the Pentecostals and other sects. It is noteworthy also that just when concern with preaching has slackened in great areas of Protestantism, many Roman Catholics are discovering with enthusiasm what is meant by the preaching of the Word. A little historical perspective, too, will show us that there have been periods of church history when the situation was infinitely more alarming than it is anywhere today (for instance, the medieval period, when many priests were entirely unequipped to preach and let the stained-glass windows and the drama tell the story; pre-Wesley eighteenth-century England; or the America of the Founding Fathers).

Our standard of comparison tends to be with the late nineteenth century, and it is worth pausing to think of certain things that have happened since then. There is no doubt whatever that the prestige of the Church and the preacher is not what it was when the thunder from a New York pulpit made saloon-keepers tremble and closed down red-light districts overnight, or when governments in

Britain could be brought down by the voice of the great Nonconformist preachers. And we are light-years away from the time when the preacher was the parson, that is to say, "the person"—one of the few educated people in the community. There has been a sea change in the social hierarchy. We may still sing in the last verse of Chesterton's magnificent hymn "O God of Earth and Altar," "Tie in a living tether/The prince and priest and thrall," but the author's medievalism can only be taken poetically in a day when the last remnants of feudalism have disappeared. Today's prayer would be to "tie in a living tether" Washington, Wall Street, the trade unions, and the media, with the Church left over as the somewhat nebulous body that does the praying. For better or for worse it is clear that the spokesmen for the Church have slipped down the totem pole.

Then the sermon today faces competition as an intellectual event in the community. There was a time when it was, in fact, about the only mental stimulus that was available, apart from the occasional lecture circuit. Professor H. R. Mackintosh once told me that in his first parish in Scotland the content of the sermon was discussed, not only over Sunday lunch, but throughout the week in the local stores, the post office, the blacksmith's shop. The newspaper and then the magazine were the first rivals for popular attention, but how much has happened in the last fifty years. Every citizen is now bombarded with material to think about. Weeklies and monthlies abound, and to them have been added the ubiquitous radio and television. (It has been reckoned that the aver-

17

age church member today has been exposed in one week to twenty minutes of preaching and nine hours of TV commercials.) Nothing less than a revolution has happened in the field of communications, and no one seems yet to have taken full account of what this has meant to the office of the preacher. It is not just that people have alternative stimulants available. It is not even that much that proceeds from the journalist, the commentator, and the TV tube is professionally on a much higher level than the average sermon. We have to reckon with the blunting effect on human sensibilities of the bombardment of news. (I have seen a roomful of diners devoting their whole attention to steak and chatter while on a screen in the corner two of our compatriots were walking on the moon.)

This is what I mean by the "age of distraction" of the chapter title. We are losing the ability to concentrate, to give our real attention to what is being said. News, commentary, sports, drama pour in upon us from all sides, and little of it is really absorbed. This is the climate in which the preacher has to find a hearing. It is another world from that in which grandfather made his way through the Sabbath calm to concentrate on the preaching of the Word.

Whether or not we agree with McLuhan's thesis that we have moved in these years from the age of print and talk to the age of the visual, there is no question that something has happened to the power of words. There has been a semantic inflation in recent years that has led to a serious devaluation of our verbal currency. Advertising has taken a tremendous toll, especially of some of the favorite expressions of the preacher. (Think what has happened to the word "important." If the preacher says he has an "important message," the congregation subconsciously switches off.) Then the inflammatory rhetoric of the champions of various causes in our generation has blunted the effect of such horrendous words as "catastrophic," "apocalyptic," "sadistic," "holocaust," "genocide," "psychotic"—not to mention such theological heavyweights as "eschatological" and "charismatic" that have been appropriated and emasculated by the secular world.

Among the words that have come down in the world is one that has special reference to the proclamation of the gospel. "Propaganda" is a perfectly good word to describe what the Church is doing in making the gospel known throughout the world. As such it has been used in the past by missionary societies like the Society for the Propagation of the Gospel, and a committee of cardinals of the Roman Church goes by the name of the Propaganda. Yet, thanks mainly to the efforts of the late Joseph Goebbels and his successors, this word has lost all shreds of respectability. Never has a generation been more sensitive to the deceptive powers of the spoken and printed word. Nobody wants to be the victim of propaganda. It is often assumed that anyone who pleads a case or a cause in public is trying to hoodwink his audience. The better the speaker, the more skilled he is in his presentation, the more he is suspected of "progaganda." We seem to have forgotten that civilization has been built on the pleading of causes and that every ethical advance at any time in history has been made possible by skilled advocacy and communicated conviction. The sermon today, therefore, has to face

19

a new hurdle. More than ever in the past the preacher is suspected, consciously or unconsciously, of being a special pleader, trying to "put something over." It is notorious that oratory as such is particularly suspect. This generation has acquired the peculiar notion that a speaker who has taken great pains to prepare his material and delivers it with persuasive power is *ipso facto* insincere, while the stumbling, ill-prepared, stammering approach is a sign of great sincerity. The acceptance of this notion has had a devastating effect on a whole generation of preachers.

The preacher's confidence has also been undermined by the modern resistance to anything in the nature of religious dogmatism. At a time when dogmatism abounds in the fields of advertising, politics, and art, the dogmatic preacher is apt to encounter a silent or spoken "Says who?" The result has been a noticeable reluctance on the part of preachers to emulate the prophetic "Thus saith the Lord." I suspect that ecclesiastical academics have exaggerated the popular resistance to dogmatism (there are no signs that Billy Graham's reiterated "The Bible says" has left him without an audience!), but preachers have been left with the feeling that they must qualify every expression of conviction, and indeed that the day of the monologue from the pulpit is over. Hence the current (or passing?) demand for dialogue, forums, and endless discussion. It is a thesis of this book that the sermon must leave its position of isolation and circulate freely in the minds of the listeners; but that does not imply an abandonment of the essential "dogma" to be proclaimed. Paul was by no means an isolated preacher. He was open to constant interruption, and his sermons flowed freely out into the marketplace. Yet his word was, "This is a faithful saying, and worthy of all acceptation, that Christ Jesus came into the world to save sinners." It was not, "This is an interesting proposition, and worthy of endless discussion, that the Christ-event has some kind of relevance to our situation of alienation."

These and other factors that have worked against the traditional acceptance of preaching in this part of the world are compounded by the crisis of confidence within the Church herself. Instead of accepting them as a challenge to rethink the mystery of preaching in the light of modern conditions, the Protestant churches have tended to downgrade the sermon as a relic of an outmoded model of the Church. It has become fashionable to say that the old-style parish church with its eleven o'clock Sunday morning service has had its day and will survive only as a nostalgic haven for the elderly. The sermon, therefore, will follow this antiquated pattern into limbo. No one could be more conscious of the precarious position of the "parish church" than the pastor of a city congregation in New York, and no one could be more convinced that radical changes will probably take place. Yet I am puzzled by the readiness of the "new theologian" to write it off, and not at all impressed by what has so far emerged as a replacement. Experiments in new forms of ministry (most of them made possible by the support of the despised "parish church") are essential for a living Church, and there is a desperate need for the Church to break out of the nineteenth-century molds and confront the modern world

21

at its points of true vitality and power; but no one has yet demonstrated how the gospel can be proclaimed and lived without the gathering of Christians in some community like the "church on the corner." And the power of the sermon in that context should not be underestimated.

Unfortunately, when the sermon is seen either as a relic of the pulpiteering of another generation, or as the occasion for mild therapy for the victims of modern society, or as a futile attempt to arouse a lethargic congregation to specific social action in the community, disillusionment is apt to set in. Therefore, there has been a diversion of clerical energies to other concerns. In the name of "liturgical renewal" some have sought to create forms of worship that will enliven the Church and demonstrate its perennial capacity to satisfy and stimulate the religious needs of mankind. The rest of this book will demonstrate my sympathy with this movement and my desire to see our Protestant churches rescued from the liturgical chaos in which we have wallowed. But liturgical renewal which ignores or underplays the position of the sermon in Christian worship is doomed to failure. It is tragic that many who are gifted in devising forms of worship for today and skilled in the liturgical history of the Church have often regarded the sermon as a kind of intrusion, an unnecessary addendum to the business of worshiping God. They have thus encouraged others to escape from the homiletic task which, in any case, they were beginning to find frustrating and pointless.

A more frequent diversion of clerical energies has, of course, been the concentration on what is called the social witness and action of the Church. Here again a necessary and demanding aspect of the Church's life has diverted attention and expectation from the sermon. With the tempting slogan "Deeds not words" the eleven o'clock service has been written off as a "talking shop," and we have been told again and again that what the world is waiting for is action not sermons. It is not surprising that many a young minister finding that his congregation is not responding to his pulpit exhortations turns to those who are willing to follow him into social and political action in the name of Jesus. Once again a divorce has occurred between two aspects of the Church's life that God has joined together. The most effective social action is happening, it would be fair to say, where there is a solid foundation of congregational worship and preaching that is thoroughly integrated in the total life of the parish.

The temptation to neglect preaching in favor of liturgical renewal or social action is, of course, facilitated by the immense pressures of the ecclesiastical machine and the passion of "busyness" that afflicts our American churches. The seminarian may approach his first parish with ideals drummed into him by his teachers of homiletics and resolve to spend x number of hours per week preparing his sermons. (He has heard of that famous preacher who spent one hour working in his study for every minute speaking in the pulpit and was at the same time a faithful pastor, a devoted committeeman, and a national figure in demand all over the country—and has not yet learned that he needs to be demythologized.) The machine, however, takes over. The entries in his diary

23

contain everything but "sermon writing." He is soon easily persuaded that the sermon will have more human appeal and direct contact if he throws a few ideas together on Saturday night. After all, there are those pressing demands for discussion and for action, and those multitudes of reports to read and write.

These distractions in the world and in the Church have naturally raised the question of the survival of the sermon as the older generation has known it. The current apocalyptic mood encourages radical criticism of the pulpit as the supreme anachronism in a dying institution. The more detached the critic is from the life of any live congregation, the louder the condemnation of the sermon—usually in the name of that tired, limp, and question-begging word "relevance." (Hermann Göring once said, "When I hear anyone talk of Culture, I reach for my revolver." When I hear anyone talk of relevance, I reach for my New Testament.") What is needed is something more than a bleak assessment of the sermon in this age of whirling change and distraction. The apocalyptic mood needs to be tempered by a sense of history. "Survival" is not necessarily a word of despair. The fact is that preaching has survived in the Church through the vicissitudes of two thousand years, including periods fully as inhospitable as our own. The Roman Church is constantly reminding us that the Vatican thinks in centuries, not years, and it would be well for all Christians to cultivate something of this habit of thought. Those who speak of the demise of the sermon probably have in mind nothing more than the obvious fact that the typical sermon of fifty years ago is

unlikely to speak to the Atomic Age. The sermon as such
—the verbal proclamation of the Good News of Jesus
Christ—survives and will survive, because it belongs to the
enduring mystery and commission of the gospel.

This is not meant to sound like an echo of the wise, but
slightly cynical, old gentleman whom I conceive as the
writer of Ecclesiastes: "The thing that hath been, it is that
which shall be; and that which is done is that which shall
be done: and there is no new thing under the sun." (We
might do worse, however, than turn to this book occasion
ally as a counterbalance to the apocalyptic excitement of
the Revelation.) This is not a time for complacent conviction that all is well with the preaching office of the Church
and that we just have to wait for the wheel to turn and
the pews will be packed again. My plea is for an open-
eyed assessment of the changed conditions and the strength
of the distractions, and for an acceptance of the challenge
based on a profound belief in the enduring mystery of
preaching. To believe in Christ is to believe in the neces-
sity and the possibility of communicating his gospel in
every age.

If we were less hypnotized by the present and the im-
mediate past, we should see more clearly how the sermon
has endured in a multitude of forms in a vast variety of
social conditions for about two thousand years. It is rooted,
of course, in the New Testament evidence. The first act
of the Christian Church, as reported in the account of
Pentecost in the second chapter of the Acts, was a sermon.
The same book makes it clear that the spectacular advance
of the gospel in the most discouraging environment was

due to the constant proclamation of the message, formally, informally, to Jew and to Gentile, throughout the imperial territory of the western Mediterranean. The spread of the gospel is inconceivable without the spoken word—addressed to the unbeliever to convince him and to the believer to strengthen him, and to the Church to urge her to "edify," build up in the faith. The epistles obviously contain material that was delivered in the form of sermons in the young churches. Behind this confidence of the apostles in the power of the spoken word lies their memory of Jesus himself, whose mission began, as Mark reports, with preaching: "Now after that John [another preacher] was put in prison, Jesus came into Galilee preaching the gospel of the kingdom of God." No one could read the New Testament and conclude that the sermon is an optional or marginal activity of the Church, or miss the note of divine mystery in the proclamation of the Word of God in the language and imagery of the day. In the New Testament the sermon is neither a pep talk nor a lecture nor an ephemeral commentary. It is the Word made flesh in contemporary language. It is a vehicle of the Spirit whereby the Real Presence of Christ is realized.

It takes little imagination to dart across the centuries and see the Christian sermon operating in astonishingly different situations. The Church Fathers were preachers, and by the time of Chrysostom ("the Golden Mouth") the sermon was a power in the land. If the medieval Church was centered on the seven sacraments and was deficient in a powerful preaching ministry, yet the pulpit remained prominent in the churches, backed by a crucifix to remind the congregation that the preacher's task is to proclaim Christ crucified. It was the voice of preaching that constantly interrupted the flow of the Church's life in the static and often corrupt periods of its temporal power. Bernard of Clairvaux, Francis of Assisi, Savonarola are only a few of the names that come to mind. Then, as everybody knows, the Reformation came in on a tide of preaching, and the sixteenth and seventeenth centuries demonstrate the power of the pulpit in that age of violent change and revolution. From the thunders of John Knox in St. Giles' to the learned, poetic, and passionate oratory of John Donne in St. Paul's, this era offers amazing examples of the survival, revival, and incandescence of the pulpit after centuries when its voice was muted. Since then the preaching of the Word has waxed and waned in the churches, but every age has seen new varieties—the open-air campaigns of John Wesley, the lay preaching of Wilberforce against slavery, the stupendous "missionary century" (1810-1910) with its expansion of the Church across the world and new methods of proclaiming the gospel, the mass meetings of modern evangelism, the advent of radio and television and their use by the preacher. The story is one of "survival" in the most positive sense, and some such perspective is necessary when we talk of survival today.

Since preaching in the biblical sense means using the language and imagery of the day in order to convey the eternal gospel, it is obvious that one task of the preacher must be to speak that language and use the imagery that is current. So part of this book will deal with the question of "our words." We shall have to ask if we are really

27

proclaiming the gospel in the language of everyday and if we really understand the things that are happening in the realm of symbolism and imagery. It may be that a revolution is required in the style and shape of the sermon. It is only too possible that those of us who preach have become entangled in a "churchy" language and an established form that have nothing to do with the eternal gospel. We should face this task with a sense of elation rather than concluding that preaching is now an impossible endeavor. The true humility of the preacher does not come from a sense of despair in face of the distractions of our world. It comes rather from a sense of the utter inadequacy of our human minds and words really to declare the Word of the living God. Every true preacher will have his moments, like Jeremiah, when he has to say, "Ah, Lord God! behold, I cannot speak: for I am a child." But the Lord, you may remember, answered, "Say not, I am a child: for thou shalt go to all that I shall send thee." He will remember that he is "sent from God." And when, again, he sometimes feels like giving up and like Jeremiah wants to say, "I will not make mention of him, nor speak any more in his name," he will surely have to add quickly, "But his word was in mine heart as a burning fire shut up in my bones, and I was weary with forbearing, and I could not stay."

Ultimately, then, the survival of preaching in an age of distraction does not depend on our acquiring new techniques or learning really to speak in the language of today. It will survive because it is the God-appointed sacrament of the Word, whereby in every age, and in an infinite variety of ways, Christ has come, converting the unbeliever and fortifying his disciples. I believe, therefore, that the recovery of nerve in the Protestant pulpit and the discovery of the Spirit's power for our day is a *theological* and not a sociological or psychological question. So we must consider first the theological backbone of the man "sent from God."

2

The Theological Backbone
of the Preacher

"In the beginning was the Word"

When we think of preaching as mystery, we are restoring it to its proper place in the enduring life of the Church. It is not the attempt to sow religious ideas in the virgin soil of a contemporary audience. It is not a moral prod to the conscience. Nor is it merely an interpretation of the contents of the Bible to the modern world by a part-time scholar with a little Greek and less Hebrew. Still less is it an effort to provide a little mild therapy for the victims of tension and strain. (Jeremiah dealt with that one when he said of the false prophets, "They have healed also the hurt of the daughter of my people slightly, saying, Peace, peace; when there is no peace.") And it is certainly not an occasion for a clergyman to air his opinions on everything from the price of meat to thermonuclear war. All these things may legitimately happen in the course of a sermon

—religious ideas may be imparted, some moralizing will be inevitable, the Bible may be interpreted, our neuroses may be relieved, statements of social or political opinion may be made—but the sermon is something else. It is an event in which an individual and a community are confronted with the Word of God. It is a mystery in which human words, in the tones and overtones of contemporary speech, become the vehicle of the living and eternal Christ.

Preaching, however, is *not* a mystery in the sense of mumbo jumbo or hocus-pocus. It is all too possible for a preacher to cast a spell over an audience by the use of all the tricks in the arsenal of demagoguery—rapid-fire, authoritative projection of logical absurdities, stirring up of latent prejudices, bamboozling the crowd with claims to esoteric information, creating an aura of mystic rapture signifying nothing. Luke tells us in the book of the Acts that one of these spiritual demagogues was active in Samaria at the time of Peter's mission in that area. "A certain man called Simon," he wrote, ". . . bewitched the people of Samaria, giving out that himself was some great one." Curiously, the man responded to Peter's preaching, and was baptized. But then it occurred to him that Peter was really nothing more than a superior kind of mystery-maker, and he offered Peter cash if he would tell him the secret. Peter's reply, in J. B. Phillips' version, was a rough one—"To hell with you and your money!" (a text I have never yet dared to use on Budget Sunday). It is interesting that "hocus-pocus" is etymologically a description of the perversion of the true mystery. During the period when the medieval Mass was at its most debased, and little was heard by a congregation except some mumbling up at the altar, the Latin words of consecration, *"Hoc est corpus meum,"* were heard as "hocus-pocus," and the supreme mystery of Christian worship had become a mere mystification. In the same way exactly, the mystery of Christian preaching can degenerate into mystification when the sermon ceases to be the vehicle for the Real Presence of Christ and becomes a spellbinder for the confusion of a congregation and the benefit of the preacher.

If, then, preaching is mystery, it can only be understood theologically. For theology is the science of the Word of God. It is the reflection of the Church on the very thing that happens when a man declares the gospel of the Scriptures in the language and the atmosphere of today. From the beginning theology has been, with notorious deviations, an attempt to think through the content of Scripture and its ongoing proclamation in the Church. Paul was a preacher before he was a theologian, and as the Epistle to the Romans shows, his theology kept pace with his preaching. In recent years we have suffered from a divorce between those whom God hath joined together. A theological generation that grew tired of, and began to despise, that not always attractive old lady, the preaching Church, soon fell into the clutches of the seductive sisters, modern pragmatism and atheism, and spawned all kinds of heresies —most of which, incidentally, had had their fling before the fourth century A.D. At the same time, the preacher, baffled and bemused by the productions of the seminary, tended to shy away from what he was told was mere "God-talk" and devoted himself to moralizing, psycholo-

32

gizing, and the manifestos of social action. It would be salutory to remember that the most massive, the most erudite, and by far the most comprehensive work of modern theology—the *Dogmatics* of Karl Barth—sprang from the author's concern with the preaching of the Word.

By the "theological backbone" of preaching in the chapter title I mean the conception a preacher has of his task: that he is one who dares to speak in public in the name of God. If the thought that this is indeed a daunting, a humanly impossible task has never entered his head, then he has no theology of preaching but only a vague desire to sound off on the subject of religion. If he is, in any sense, awed by the mystery of what he is doing, caught up in the strange compulsion of the prophet—"his word was in mine heart as a burning fire shut up in my bones, and I was weary with forbearing, and I could not stay"—then he knows that behind what he is doing lies a theology, a conception of the mysterious relationship between God and man, some kind of understanding of what is meant by Holy Scripture, Holy Spirit, and the grace of the Lord Jesus Christ.

As a preacher with a dated theological education, supplemented by sporadic reading of the new voices, and illumined by personal and pastoral experiences in various countries in peace and war, let me try to express, however crudely, the kind of theological convictions that have lain behind my preaching. I do so without any pretension to even such a modified kind of infallibility as Professor Hans Küng now allows the Pope, without any suggestion that every preacher ought to think just *so* about the nature

33

of his task, and without implying that having reached certain theological convictions about forty years ago I have held them unmodified ever since.

For me the very possibility of preaching is rooted in the doctrine of the Holy Trinity. There is the ultimate mystery —not, as so many seem to think, the mystification—of the Christian faith. From that mystery derives the mystery of preaching. Obviously, insofar as the doctrine of the Trinity attempts to describe the indescribable—the inner nature of God himself—we are in the realm of the ineffable, which is to say that at this point we do not describe, but sing, "Holy, Holy, Holy, is the Lord of hosts: the whole earth is full of his glory." But the thought of the Trinity contains something more than impenetrable mystery: it is, in fact, a realization that the God whom we cannot describe is a communicating God, a living God, a God who has within himself that which corresponds to our experience of self-communication.

From now on let me anchor myself in that astonishing, exhilarating, and constantly seminal passage of Scripture known as the Prologue to the Gospel of St. John.

"In the beginning was the Word." It is not accidental that the first three words take us back to the Genesis statement that has survived all the assaults of its enemies and the misguided protection of its friends: "In the beginning . . . God." That is the basic statement of the theology of creation. The words "in the beginning" stand like a frontier —what the Germans call a *Grenzbegriff*—beyond which we cannot go. John says (let me call him John without worrying whether this may indeed have been written by another gentleman with the same name) that this creative God is creative from the beginning, creative, as it were, within himself before there was anything else. "In the beginning was the Word." How else can you say it? This is a communicating God, a God in whom there is from all eternity that which we know as "communion." A preacher, therefore, is not one who points to some lone Absolute, an unmoved and unmoving divine Unity, with whom or with which we may or may not be able to establish some kind of relationship, but the witness to a living God who, whether or not we want to call him or her *a* Person, is to an infinite degree that which we call *personal.* "When all things began," reads the New English Bible, "the Word already was." "At the beginning," translates Phillips, "God expressed himself."

To say that the Word was in the beginning is to believe in a God who expresses himself, and it is that self-expression, that eternal communication, which the doctrine of the Trinity symbolizes. Then comes the thought of God's expressing himself in creation: "All things were made by him; and without him was not any thing made that was made." This is, if you like, the outward movement of the living God. What is reflected here is the Genesis picture of the Spirit of God moving "upon the face of the waters"—the dark, chaotic waters that covered an earth "without form, and void." Now there emerges the thought of God's communication with his human family: "In him was life; and the life was the light of men." The same Spirit who wrought upon the chaos to make the cosmos is seeking to bring life and direction to the human family.

Here we need the newer translation: "The light shines on in the dark, and the darkness has never mastered it" (NEB). What I hear in these words is the assertion of the enduring presence of the Spirit of God, the wind of the Spirit constantly blowing through the story of mankind, moving men and women toward a communion with their God and a realization of their true life in him. This was the thought that Paul echoed in Athens when he spoke of God having "made of one blood all nations of men for to dwell on all the face of the earth . . . ; That they should seek the Lord, if haply they might feel after him, and find him, though he be not far from every one of us: For in him we live, and move, and have our being." There is a majestic universality at this point in the Prologue which should exclude the troubling thought that the entire human race lies in total darkness until the Church comes along with the story of Bethlehem and Calvary.

Now comes the shock. From the soaring conception of a living, self-communicating God, who expresses himself in creation and in the story of a human family with whom he desires a communion that must depend on their response, we come abruptly to the solid, flesh-and-blood figure of a man we know. Enter the preacher—the subject of these lectures: "There was a man sent from God, whose name was John." The transition is so abrupt that many have been tempted to look on these verses as an interpolation. If you remove them the Prologue reads beautifully and remains in the atmosphere of eternal truth—the Spirit of God, the Word of God, seeking the response of mankind: "All that came to be was alive with his life, and that life was the light of men. The light shines on in the dark, and the darkness has never mastered it. . . . He was in the world; but the world, though it owed its being to him, did not recognize him. He entered his own realm, and his own would not receive him. But to all who did receive him, to those who have yielded him their allegiance, he gave the right to become the children of God" (NEB). All this is said about the eternal Word, the communicating Spirit of God.

I believe, however, that the intervening verses are not the intrusive work of some disciple of John the Baptist. The author deliberately brings onto the stage the figure of the preacher, the man "sent from God." This is the pre-Christian preacher, the Old Testament prophet, as we would say, who is the forerunner of the herald of the gospel. It is through him that men hear of the Word and will of the Father-God. He speaks human language. He talks of mundane things—like giving away a coat, if you have two; not playing tricks with your taxes; and avoiding violence. "In the beginning was the Word . . ." Begin there, we are being told, with your theology of preaching, but you are bound to end with the specific, all too human figure of the preacher, the man "sent from God." Or, if you like, begin with the preacher—and the moment you take seriously the words "sent from God" you are led back to the thought of the eternal communicating God. Between the words "In the beginning was the Word" and "There was a man sent from God" lies the whole theology of preaching.

Right here the function and the status of the preacher

are defined, whether we are talking about an Old Testament prophet or someone who mounts a pulpit in Manhattan in 1973. In the Bible the prophet is not seen as a man of religious genius. The secular historian may classify the sixth-century prophets of Israel with other figures of that extraordinary epoch and speak about a remarkable outcropping of brilliant thinkers with unique moral insight. The Bible simply sees them as men "sent from God" with no other claim to attention than that they are witnesses to him. Preachers in modern times have—with diminishing frequency—been referred to as men of outstanding gifts, princes of the pulpit, trumpeters of righteousness, orators of morality, and the like. The true nature of the preacher is here simply described: "He came as a witness to testify to the light, that all might become believers through him. He was not himself the light; he came to bear witness to the light" (NEB). These words might well be inscribed in the pulpit where every preacher can see them: "He was not himself the light; he came to bear witness to the light." The witness to the Word of God is given in the stumbling, ordinary, contemporary words of men.

But John the Baptist was not a Christian preacher. You remember the enigmatic words of Jesus: "Among them that are born of women there hath not risen a greater than John the Baptist; notwithstanding he that is least in the kingdom of heaven is greater than he." Does this not mean that a new world has dawned with the gospel of Christ, and that the preacher who gave witness to the Light in terms of the law and the prophets will be followed by the preacher who points to the revelation of God's overwhelming grace in the crucified and risen Lord? This is what the artist Grünewald saw as he painted the Isenheim altarpiece in which he introduces the figure of John the Baptist standing beside the cross with a long finger pointing to the divine victim—"Behold the Lamb of God, which taketh away the sin of the world."

The climax of John's Prologue comes, of course, with the fourteenth verse: "The Word was made flesh, and dwelt among us . . . full of grace and truth." This, we are being told, is what the ensuing narrative is all about. It presents to us Jesus, the flesh-and-blood Jesus who lives our human life in all its ecstasies and agonies, totally vulnerable yet utterly responsive to the Spirit of God. Now we are no longer hearing about a divine Word dimly echoed in the words of the prophet, nor of a witness to the Light. This *is* the Word, alive in flesh and blood: this *is* the Light, shining, as Paul once put it, with "the glory of God in the face of Jesus Christ." Jesus is thus more than a messenger of God, more than "a man sent from God." He is the Divine Presence in human terms: he is *"the* man sent from God." The Prologue is telling us that the God whose revelation was reflected in the human words of the law and the prophets has made an unimaginable revelation of himself in the living, breathing, speaking, suffering person of Jesus Christ. As the writer to the Hebrews put it: "When in former times God spoke to our forefathers, he spoke in fragmentary and varied fashion through the prophets. But in this final age he has spoken to us in the Son . . . who is the effulgence of God's splendour and the stamp of God's very being" (NEB). It is to this Jesus, the personal revelation of God, and the bearer of his grace—the Word translated into human terms—that the Christian preacher has to bear witness. And in doing so he relies on the apostolic testimony as recorded here: "We beheld his glory."

What we find in the Prologue as the theological backbone of the preacher is thus a kind of symphony on the theme of the Word of God. Without being too schematic I might express it somewhat like this: We believe in a living God in whom the Word—communication—is eternally present as Father, Son, and Holy Spirit; this outgoing God brings the world into being and in that world seeks communion with his human family through the light of his Spirit: at one specific point in time he made the supreme revelation as "the Word was made flesh and dwelt among us." Those who "beheld his glory" have left the record of what happened: and thus the preacher today is enabled to proclaim the Word as one "sent from God" and to "bear witness of the Light." Hence for those with tidy minds (and no mystery such as we are dealing with can really be tidily expressed) one might formulate the sequence: the eternal Word (the Holy Trinity)—the living Word (Jesus Christ)—the written Word (the contemporary witness to Jesus, along with the tradition of the law and the prophets out of which he came)—the spoken Word (the words of the contemporary preacher).

I once heard a simple statement about the Trinity which still seems to me illuminating: it was to the effect that we can think of God the Father as "God everywhere and always"; God the Son as "God there and then"; and God the Holy Spirit as "God here and now." With that in mind one could say that the sermon as the word "here and now" is totally dependent on the presence of the Spirit. One can talk about the God of "everywhere and always" without engaging anything more than the intellectual curiosity of the hearers (and be lucky to have even that). One can talk about the historic Jesus in such a way as to leave the impression of infinite distance between him and us, or to imply that he left little more than a moral code for our guidance. But when the Holy Spirit is present the eternal God and the living Christ are suddenly contemporary. Here and now God is speaking, and through contemporary words the Word of God comes into action.

So we return to the central mystery by which human words, spoken words— eloquent or faltering, logical or lyrical, premeditated or spontaneous, wise or foolish—can become the vehicle of the Word of God, the Real Presence of Christ. If this sketch of a theological backbone for preaching is in any sense valid, it points up the need for strong conviction about what one might call both the *divinity* and *humanity* of the sermon. By that I mean a belief that the living God still speaks, that he does reveal himself to the man and woman of 1973, that the divine moment is really there in a service of contemporary worship, combined with an equally strong belief that the words to be used by the preacher must be really, honestly, and totally the words that normal people use today. Modern preaching is weak either where there is no real belief that a living God seeks personal communication with all of us, or where all kinds of special churchy language are used in an attempt to convey some kind of fuzzy impression that one is being religious.

Just as there have always been heresies in the Church concerning the person of Christ—called heresies because they denied the Catholic doctrine that Jesus is both fully human and fully divine—so there are homiletical heresies which offer a conception of the sermon which is neither fully human nor fully divine. The heresies in the early Church were condemned because they left their adherents with a view of Jesus as one who was neither God nor man but some kind of creature in between. A lot of sermons come under the category of some kind of creature in between. You don't get the impression that the preacher really believes that God may indeed be speaking in and through his words, nor do you get the impression that you are hearing the kind of language a contemporary politician, journalist, or lecturer might use. The preacher is a "man sent from *God*"—therefore, he must be conscious of the divine commission, and the divine event, the authoritative Scripture from which he speaks, and the presence of the Spirit here and now. But the preacher is also the *"man* sent from God"—and not some creature from the twilight world of man's incurable religiosity.

What this theological backdrop does for the sermon of today needs some examination. If some such apprehension of the enduring mystery of preaching is true to the evidence of the New Testament and the experience of the

Church, we shall have to think hard about the place and function of the sermon in the Church of today and tomorrow. Preacher and preached-to will have to review their ingrained habits and be responsive to the unexpected prompting of the Spirit, who is God truly "here and now."

3

How to Listen to a Sermon

"What will this babbler say?"

When a man "sent from God" known as Paul of Tarsus came to Athens, the intellectual capital of the Empire, he was not exactly received as a distinguished visiting preacher. There were no expectant Christian congregations waiting to be stirred by his apostolic words, nor any pool of unattached Christians to swell the crowds at the services. This was virgin territory for the gospel, and Paul plunged in with his usual zest to deliver the Word of the living God. He followed his normal tactics, making first for the synagogue and arguing his case with his fellow Jews. Normally, he found two totally different audiences in the cities he visited: the Jews and the large number of Gentiles who had been attracted to the tenets of Judaism; and the masses who were, in one way or another, under the influence of the fading gods and goddesses of the ancestral cults. He went to the synagogue first, since there he found a certain common language. These were people who knew roughly what was meant by "the Word of God," and by such words as "sin," "salvation," "sacrifice," and "kingdom of God." They also knew what it was to listen to a sermon, and—let us note—to follow it up with a lively disputation. (Today we call it "forum" or "feedback" and think we have invented something new. Jesus in his hometown of Nazareth and Paul in the synagogues of Asia Minor both experienced "feedbacks" that would make the modern preacher run for cover.) Paul's approach to the pagans was entirely different, and we find that one of his troubles as a man "sent from God" was how to avoid being welcomed as a god himself. Apparently what we would call his "charisma" was such that the ordinary pagans who heard him were conscious of a supernatural presence and power even when they didn't understand a word he was saying. He had to grope for words that would make it clear that "he was not himself the light; he came to bear witness to the light."

In Athens Paul found himself confronted by a third group, one that he was not familiar with in the normal course of his mission, but with which he felt entirely able to grapple. This was the coterie of sophisticates, the intellectuals who had nothing but contempt for the ancient religions, tended toward one or other of the rival philosophical schools of the Stoics and Epicureans, delighted in abstract argumentation, and collected new ideas and exotic terminology as a lepidopterist pursues butterflies. Some of these overheard Paul when he was holding forth in the

45

public forum that resembled Speakers' Corner in London's Hyde Park. Luke dryly reports, "Then certain philosophers of the Epicureans, and of the Stoics, encountered him. And some said, What will this babbler say?" (If you prefer the contemporary diction of a modern translation to the robust language of King James' committee, the New English Bible has, "And some of the Epicurean and Stoic philosophers joined issue with him. Some said, 'What can this charlatan be trying to say?' " One way or the other, it's the response of the supersophisticated seminarian who tunes in to Billy Graham by mistake.)

Luke also notes that these people listened long enough to overhear the constant repetition of two words—in Greek, *Jesus* and *Anastasis* ("resurrection"). This reveals, incidentally, the basic content of Paul's preaching at this time—Jesus and the Resurrection—but in the snap judgment of the passing philosophers it sounded like the heralding of two new gods: "He seemeth to be a setter forth of strange gods [they said]: because he preached unto them Jesus and the resurrection." (Or, " 'He would appear to be a propagandist for foreign deities' "—this because he was preaching about Jesus and Resurrection" [NEB].) So, in the end, Paul received a polite invitation to expound his views before the distinguished company of the Court of Areopagus. These cultured pagans may have proposed to shoot him down, but at least they knew enough about listening to a sermon to be prepared to give the preacher a chance.

It's not my purpose now to analyze the famous sermon of which Luke obviously gives us only an extract. I would simply record my view that it was not the disaster exegetes have often described it as being. Paul did adopt a new style, complete with philosophical references and quotes from the Greek poets, but the word "Resurrection" made its appearance— and the gauntlet of the gospel was flung down. We are told that "when they heard about the raising of the dead, some scoffed; and others said, 'We will hear you on this subject some other time.' However, some men joined him and became believers, including Dionysius, a member of the Court of Areopagus; also a woman named Damaris, and others besides" (NEB). I would settle for that as a result of my Easter sermon.

My topic now is not the style of preaching suitable for such an audience, but how to listen to a sermon. While I have in mind chiefly the attitude of a regular congregation, we might think for a moment about the kind of people described in this passage. Obviously one cannot lecture a total skeptic who has eliminated religion as a subject worthy of serious consideration on the correct frame of mind with which to hear the Christian evangel. But I have long since given up the habit of segregating my neighbors into neat little categories labeled atheist, agnostic, semi-agnostic, semi-believer, believer. If I seemed to be doing so in my description of these Athenian intellectuals, I apologize to them—for among them were not only the scoffers, but the curious and those two fascinating "convertibles," Dionysius (what a wonderful name for a new Christian!) and Damaris. It is part of one's belief in the sacrament of preaching that no human being is beyond reach; and it ought to be part of the strategy of the Church not to dismiss any human being as psychologically immune to the gospel.

Our tendency to view mankind from our ecclesiastical ghetto and to perceive three categories—members, the fringe, and nonmembers—blinds us to the fact that response to the Word of God has infinite gradations. The scoffer, the curious ("We will hear you on this subject another time"), and the believers are not located respectively outside the Church, on the fringe, and inside. They are all over the place, and indeed may all three be present in any one of us. The temper of our times is such that it is less than ever possible to drop anyone into his religious slot. There was a time when people used to talk of a "Christian country," meaning that everyone was really a regular believer in God, with the exception of a few pockets of arrogant atheism. This was succeeded by a time when it was fashionable to talk of "the Post-Christian Age," meaning that everybody was really an atheist, with the exception of a few pockets of arrogant believers. We surely know now that neither picture resembles the truth. We are living in a time of enormous religious confusion, and considerable religious vitality. Not only have the denominational labels ceased to indicate in most cases any easily identifiable loyalty, but there is an increasing cross-traffic between Protestant, Catholic, and Jew. Beneath the surface of the old categories lurk an incredible variety of beliefs and doubts. The wedding guest who confesses that he's never been in a church before may reveal intense spiritual convictions, while the church officer may on occasion lay bare some fundamental disbelief. Age has nothing to do with it. The young hippie may turn out to be a fundamentalist, while the old lady may tell you (as one did recently to me) that she "doesn't" believe a word of it."

In these circumstances, I feel that it is possible to make at least one or two suggestions to the skeptic about listening to a sermon. To the utterly closed-minded atheist, perhaps dragged to church to attend a funeral (where he is at least exposed to the gospel in Scripture and in prayer), I could only say what Cromwell did to the equally hard ened Scottish Presbyterians with whom he had to deal: "I beseech you, in the bowels of Christ, conceive it possible that you may be mistaken." But to all others I would plead for the recognition that a sermon—even a poor sermon—might just possibly be a means of glimpsing that alluring territory of the Spirit for which the Post-materialist Age is so obviously groping.

I would ask the skeptic in the pew or at the receiving end of a religious broadcast to listen to a sermon with an openness to the dimension of mystery and not merely with the critical judgment of the mind. This is not to suggest that anyone should unplug his intellectual equipment, so to speak, at the church door, but that he should raise the antenna by which we all are made sensitive to realities that cannot be captured by the mind. We do not listen to poetry or music with the intellect alone, and a sermon, though by no means always a work of art, can appeal to a consciousness or intuition that transcends the faculty of reason. Coleridge spoke of "that willing suspension of disbelief for the moment, which constitutes poetic faith."

Religious faith does not demand a renunciation of our normal faculties of judgment, nor is it "for the moment"; but something in the nature of a "willing suspension of disbelief" is required in anyone who is to be reached by the Word that transcends all human words, anyone who is willing to be grasped by the divine. The requirement is simply an abstinence from the dogmatism that rules out any revelation that transcends our normal experience of the world around us and the conventional logic of our minds.

This is not to say that intellectual garbage should not be recognized as intellectual garbage, that sentimental nonsense, and the arrogance of ignorance, should not be seen for what they are. It simply means that a sermon should not only be judged on its merits as a well-argued proposition, but be given the chance to convey a Word, to communicate a truth, to be the vehicle for an experience, that lies beyond the normal workings of the mind. In the enduring mystery of preaching it has often happened that men and women of exceptional intellectual brilliance have been, like C. S. Lewis, "surprised by joy"—the joy of the gospel mediated through the most simple, crude, or banal words or events. A sermon is much more than a series of propositions offered for acceptance. It is an appeal "sent from God" that moves in the mysterious area where we communicate in depth.

We have been thinking of the sermon as evangelism, as the means whereby we hear and respond to the Word of God in Christ, and I have dared to suggest a frame of mind with which the skeptic might listen. When we consider the sermon not as an instrument of evangelism (whether in the course of regular worship or on radio or television, or the mass meeting) but rather as an integral part of the worship of the Church, the question of listening becomes all-important. Quite clearly, the preaching moment is not a kind of interruption of the worship of God in order to flash an appeal to the unconverted. It may well be that we have muted the evangelistic note for too long in our churches and that the call to make a decision for Christ ought to be heard more frequently, but the sermon is certainly not the point at which the flock sits back to listen to an attempt to make a few black sheep white.

The New Testament speaks of preaching the Word not only as proclamation of the gospel but also as a means of building up a congregation in the faith. From the beginning the apostles and their successors saw their preaching task as twofold: making known the gospel to the unbeliever; and strengthening, instructing, inspiring, and guiding the Church of God. The book of the Acts reports that when Paul said his farewell to the elders of the church at Ephesus he concluded, "And now, brethren, I commend you to God, and to *the word of his grace,* which is able to build you up, and to give you an inheritance among all them which are sanctified." It was "the word of his grace," expounded in the course of worship, that enabled these early Christians to hold fast, and to grow. When Paul wrote to the Corinthian Church at the time of a controversy about *Glossolalia*—speaking in tongues—he drew a distinction between this particular gift of the Spirit and preaching: "When a man is using the language of ecstasy

51

he is talking with God, not with men, for no man understands him; he is no doubt inspired, but he speaks mysteries. On the other hand, when a man prophesies [preaches], he is talking to men, and his words have *power to build;* they stimulate and they encourage" (NEB). The King James Version has here, "He that prophesieth speaketh unto men to edification, and exhortation, and comfort." "Edification" is somehow a good word gone wrong. It sounds rather smug to our ears, but literally it just means "building up." That is a function of the sermon in Christian worship.

As part of the rhythm of a service the sermon belongs to the movement from God to us that we call the "hearing of the Word." Liturgically it belongs there, to be followed by a congregation's response in offering, thanksgiving, and dedication—the movement from us to God. It does not belong at the very end of the service as a kind of climactic event. Nor is it the moment at which the congregation ceases to participate actively and settles back to be stimulated, interested, instructed—or entertained. It is, or ought to be, so thoroughly integrated into the movement of worship that preacher and congregation are actively sharing in the sacrament of the Word.

An essential factor, then, in listening to a sermon is the faith of both preacher and hearer. Just as, according to our doctrine of the Holy Communion, the bread and wine only become for us the Body and Blood of Christ only when faith is present, so, in the sacrament of the Word, human words remain just human words without the faith of both speaker and listener. It is extremely difficult to define what is meant by the presence of this animating faith in a congregation, but every sensitive preacher is aware of it—or of its absence. Modern homiletics, obsessed with the techniques of the preacher, has neglected this aspect of the sermon. When preaching to a strange congregation one very soon senses whether there is this spirit of faith and expectancy among the listeners, or whether the prevailing mood is one of detachment, mild intellectual curiosity, or incipient boredom.

"Faith" here means expectancy—the readiness to believe that God will speak, that we shall experience the Real Presence of Christ. The preacher may, or may not, invoke the presence of the Trinity, or use such a prayer as "Let the words of my lips and the meditation of our hearts be acceptable in thy sight, O Lord, our strength and our redeemer," but this is the atmosphere of shared faith in which authentic preaching takes place. Much has been said about a sermon being "truth through personality," about the unique importance at this point in worship of the character of the preacher; yet in the theology of the Word there is room for the thought that God may speak, not only through, but in spite of, the preacher. It is orthodox Roman Catholic doctrine that you may receive a valid Communion from the hands of a rogue priest. I am not suggesting that the presence of a scoundrel in the pulpit makes no difference to your reception of a valid Word from God, but I do believe that your "edification" in Christ does not depend on your personal opinion of the preacher. The spirit of faith transcends questions of human relationships at this point. Every Sunday there must be a number of faithful worshipers being fed by the Word without having any special regard for, or even knowledge of, the personality of the preacher. The most direct and dramatic Word ever spoken to me in the course of a sermon—my call to the Christian ministry—came when I was in a church of another denomination, listening to a preacher I didn't know, and a sermon about which I remember nothing whatever.

Just as I suggested that the words "He was not himself the light; he came to bear witness to the light" might be inscribed inside every pulpit for the preacher to see, so on the outside of the pulpit, visible to the congregation, could be the words "Speak, Lord; for thy servant heareth." The renewal of worship and the revival of true preaching are dependent more on this spirit of faith and expectancy than on liturgical reforms or homiletic revolution. That is why I believe it to be a mistake to confine discussion of the sermon to the clergy as if it were purely a matter of professional competence. In the sermon the faith of the preacher and the faith of the congregation interact. It is not a solo performance, but the communal act of the Christian Church at worship. The parallel is not exact, but I imagine that doctors view the healing art as a cooperation with patients and find that a lack of faith and expectation frustrates the healing process. (The story is told of a doctor who inquired of a patient, "Well, what's wrong with you?" "That's for you to find out," the patient snapped back. Whereupon the doctor simply said, "I'm a doctor, not a veterinarian.") The preacher, faced with the demand that

54

the sermon be solely his responsibility, might answer, "I'm a preacher, not a recording."

Listening in faith and expectancy does not preclude the use of one's critical faculties. On the contrary, the preacher is greatly helped by the active listener who raises questions, voices doubts, offers amendments, either at an open forum or privately. The preacher of the Word lives with the disturbing thought that his regular congregation must suffer from his own limited understanding, his own emphases in the range of Christian truth, his own inevitable preferences in the selection of Bible passages for exposition. He needs the guidance, the insight, the experience, of the whole community of believers. It may be that the best way to ensure this is to enlist the support of a congregational group in the preliminary work of exegesis before a sermon is constructed, so that a sermon beomes much more the shared work of preacher and listener than it usually is. Even if that proves difficult to achieve for many of us, we are nevertheless dependent on the shared faith of the congregation, expressed in a hundred different ways, from the passing remark to a real baring of the soul in a moment of crisis.

Another expression of the communal nature of the sermon is, of course, the prayer of faith that accompanies the Word. Those who are to listen should join in the silent or vocal prayer with which a preacher begins. It is not a professional formula indicating that the time has come for a congregation to sit and hear something. Nor is it just a cry for help by the one in the pulpit, suddenly conscious of the inadequacy of the manuscript in front of him. It

55

is a common prayer for the illumination of the Spirit, for the coming of Christ, and it is a preparing of the mind and spirit for the word of "edification, and exhortation and comfort."

That last word reminds us that this is by far the most popular expectation among the listeners to a sermon in our age. This is one of the many points (the status of the sermon itself being among them) at which the clergy and laity seem often to be at odds. The average layman stubbornly insists that he listens to a sermon to get some comfort out of it, to have his faith strengthened, or as he says, "to have his batteries charged." Meanwhile, book after book appears, written by ministers or seminary teachers, castigating the conventional churches for peddling "comfortable words," demanding what they call "prophetic preaching"—by which is usually meant stamping as hard as one can on the theological and political corns of a typical Establishment congregation and insisting that the way to listen to a sermon is to be prepared to be infuriated. Who is right?

In the first place, I maintain that the typical layman listening to a sermon is perfectly right to expect some comfort—in its literal sense of "strengthening with" and not its debased use as sentimental head-patting or empty-headed reassurance. In other words, you listen to a sermon expecting *grace*. That is the content of the Word of God in Christ—the assurance of our acceptance, forgiveness, and renewal by the power of the Spirit. I suspect that the greatest weakness of the American pulpit today could be the absence of this note of grace—both in the fulminations of the Right and the lamentations of the Left. The one school thunders against the doctrinal lapses and moral permissiveness of the day; the other constantly bewails the "sickness" of America and seems to aim at arousing a bad conscience about everything from China to Peru. Both are moralistic and not evangelical. (I hesitate to use the word "moralistic," since I have noticed that in some quarters it is used chiefly to attack the conscience of one who disagrees with you. If your hang-up is alcoholism or the drug problem or communism, you're moralistic. If mine is the armaments industry or South Africa, I'm highly moral.) All this kind of preaching risks self-righteousness on the one hand, and a sense of hopelessness on the other. The self-righteousness creeps in when the listener approves of the stand the preacher is taking and damns the folly or apathy of those who disagree. The hopelessness is aroused by a preaching that omits the sound of God welcoming the sinner, the merriment of the Father's house as the prodigal returns; or the sound of the trumpets proclaiming the final triumph of the Crucified.

Yet, in the second place, we have to take seriously this question of "exhortation," the prophetic word that cuts into our misconceptions, prejudices, hidden guilts, and self-protective opinions. Any suggestions on how to listen to a sermon would be sadly incomplete without reference to this aspect of preaching. The question is: How do you listen to a sermon that upsets you, annoys you, threatens you, and generally makes you mad?

To coin a phrase, let me make one thing perfectly clear. You are under no obligation to accept meekly a vehement and one-sided diatribe on a social or political issue on which conscientious Christians hold differing views. You have every right to protest—not, I suggest, by muttering and wriggling in the pew, but verbally or in writing within the fellowship of the church. Similarly, anything that sounds like an unfair personal attack or vicious sideswipe should be resented. But I suggest that you are unlikely to frequent for long a church where this regularly takes place. It is, however, probable that at some time in the course of years of listening you will feel a legitimate grouch. Then, if it is serious enough, let the preacher know—the preacher first, and not everybody else.

Once we have allowed for this legitimate response by a sermon-listener to this abuse of the pulpit, we are still left with the scriptural, historical, and actual evidence that preaching is meant to disturb as well as comfort. There is no question about the effect of the preaching of the Old Testament prophets. When Amos, Isaiah, or Jeremiah began to say, "Hear the word of the Lord," it was seldom that what followed was assurances of comfort and joy. Nine times out of ten it was a direct attack on the social habits, the administration of justice, the religious ceremonies, or the foreign policy of the nation. And what was the response of those who heard? Isaiah must have roused the wrath of the Establishment, the judges, the priests, the society ladies, the State Department, and everyone else he aimed at. Amos was sent packing from the precincts of Bethel and told to go elsewhere: "O thou seer, go, flee thee away into the land of Judah, and there eat bread and prophesy there: But prophesy not again any more at Bethel: for it is the king's chapel, and it is the king's court." Jeremiah ended up in the stocks.

This is what the more radical have in mind today when they call for more "prophetic preaching." I have already indicated that I have doubts about the too simple identification of Christian preaching with the voice of the Hebrew prophet. (A seminarian once told me that he could only preach from the Old Testament and not from the New. When I asked why, he said, "Because *they* are political.") The New Testament seems to mean something different by the word "prophesying," and there is no evidence of any such direct political preaching either in the sermons of Jesus or in those of his apostles. But there is every evidence that listening to them was by no means always a comforting experience. "The word of God is alive and active," says the Epistle to the Hebrews. "It cuts more keenly than any two-edged sword, piercing as far as the place where life and spirit, joints and marrow, divide" (NEB). The preaching of Jesus, the preaching of Peter and Paul, the preaching of the Fathers of the Church, had this incisive effect. The Word of God penetrated, and habits, opinions, prejudices, personal relationships were radically changed.

This is the most difficult, yet the most necessary, element for all of us in listening to a sermon. There is resistance to any demand that real change take place in our ingrained habits or opinions. Yet if a congregation is really trained to listen for the Word of God, the note of judgment cannot be ignored.

With this conception in our minds of the sermon as an act in which the entire congregation participates, we must look at the role of the preacher today with a side-glance at a false image that is rapidly disappearing.

4

The Role of the Preacher in a Living Church Today

"Good night, sweet prince of the pulpit"

Once upon a time there was a prince of the pulpit. His throne was one of those massive, heavily decorated platforms, centrally placed with a vast wilderness of surrounding pews. The church was, in fact, constructed as an auditorium for the words of his lips. Every Sunday, after the preliminaries had been disposed of—hymns, prayers, and sundry anthems and announcements— a hush would fall on a great congregation; they had come, and the prince would launch into the sermon. For half an hour or more he would dazzle, cajole, expound, denounce, encourage; with perhaps a closing hymn, he pronounced a benediction and disappeared. Few were ever permitted to follow him in order to discover the answer to that fascinating question once raised in an essay of Beverley Nichols on great men: "Are they the same at home?" The next morning the newspapers would headline the event and quote at length some of the more sensational passages. During the week, his opinions would be sought on the great issues of the day. Important committees would await his presence. Politicians would seek his endorsement or try to avert his wrath. Publishers would clamor for his manuscripts. Saloon-keepers and brothel owners would tremble with rage and anxiety at the sound of his name. And the prince would bask in the praise and plaudits of the Christian community—and even of his fellow clergy.

A caricature? Yes—for who could dismiss with such a shrug the great preachers of America, of Scotland, or of the high holy days of English Nonconformity? There *were* giants whose insight, eloquence, knowledge of the Scriptures, and homiletical courage are part of our heritage in the Church Universal. At times we, their successors, are so overawed by their stature that we are made to feel like pip-squeaks in the pulpit. For who has not heard of the great Dr. X, who spent forty hours working on every half-hour sermon, who was in demand across the country at conventions of all kinds, who consulted with the mighty and yet was always on call for the most humble, who served on national committees but assiduously visited the homes of his people. Well, Dr. X, as I have said, needs to be demythologized. For our comfort we need to be told there never was such a person. Yet, once the prince of the pulpit has been cut down to size, we still acknowledge a very considerable stature. And we have no right to justify our homiletical laziness by denigrating the pulpit orators of the past.

The point is that this period really is past, and is unlikely to return again. "Good night, sweet prince"—and I would like to add the remaining words of the quotation, "And flights of angels sing thee to thy rest!" It might occur to you that this is simply one more example of the disappearance in our day of the Great Man. Even allowing for the fact that as one grows older the illusion of the Superman begins to disappear, it is obvious that in our generation the mighty charismatic characters are in short supply—and we seem to like it that way. We have exchanged a Churchill for a Heath, a Stalin for a Brezhnev, a de Gaulle for a Pompidou, a Hitler for a Brandt—I'll stop there. The mood seems to be for effective collaboration rather than charismatic leadership, for the managerial type rather than the star. So it is in the arts and literature. No one says that they are dying, yet few great names seem to emerge. Again, business and finance don't seem to be dominated by anyone resembling the powerful names that now decorate our banks and hotels. So it might be concluded that we should expect to find no princes of the pulpit, but at best effective collaborators in the total work of the Church, adequate workmen—if you like, managerial types.

On the whole, I reject the parallel. Rather I would say that the concept of the prince of the pulpit, the prima donna, was a temporary aberration in the history of the Church, and that the sooner we say a final goodnight to this nineteenth-century image, the better.

In the first place, the concept reeks of what our Roman Catholic friends call "triumphalism." Triumphalism is the mood in which the Church seeks to dominate society and to impose her standards on the world by the sheer weight of her authority. Protestants are quick to point to examples of Catholic triumphalism in medieval Europe, in seventeenth-century France, or in modern Spain, but the charge could equally be leveled against such manifestations of clerical power as, for instance, the political clout of the so-called Nonconformist conscience in nineteenth-century England—not to mention the more blatantly political interventions of John Knox, the "thundering Scot" in the pulpit of St. Giles'. It is a perennial temptation for the preacher in periods of church ascendancy to forget that he is called to be, not a prince of the pulpit, but a servant of the Word.

Secondly, the image suggests in many ways that subtle heresy, discovered by the post-Stalin Communists, known as the "cult of personality." Heaven knows, we need men and women of personality in the pulpit, and heaven preserve us from a generation of preachers who are content to deliver at second hand the material of other men funneled through some weekly sermon-service. But there is something wrong when the worship of Almighty God comes to be described as "going to hear Dr. X," and Dr. X's personal prejudices come to loom larger than the Word of Scripture. The preacher is indeed a man or a woman "sent from God"—and the God-given personality is not to be dimmed by the assumption of an inhuman, impersonal, official manner or tone of voice. (In an elocution class I attended as a seminarian one of my colleagues was rebuked for speaking in an artificial, somewhat nasal whine; to which criticism he replied, "Sir, I am using the official voice of the Church of Scotland.") A preacher must be himself, but it should be a self at the service of the Word of God. The Prologue to the Fourth Gospel docs not open with the words "In the beginning was the man sent from God." He takes his place at the end of the line: the eternal Word; the incarnate Word; the written Word—then the "man sent from God." No one could accuse the apostle Paul of being just a "wandering voice" conveying the official teachings of the Church. The personality of the man—"warts and all"—comes glowing through his letters after two thousand years. Yet it was not mock modesty that made him catch his breath when he was writing to the Corinthians and comparing himself with other apostles—"In my labours I have outdone them all"—and add quickly, "not I, indeed, but the grace of God working with me. But what matter, I or they? This is what we all proclaim, and this is what you believed" (NEB). What they all proclaimed, what we all believe—that comes before the personality of the preacher.

Paul, Chrysostom, Augustine, Luther, Calvin, Wesley—these mighty preachers were, first of all, *churchmen* rather than pulpit orators. The isolation of the preacher as the "bright star . . . in lone splendour hung aloft the night" is an invention of the nineteenth century. We are suffering now from the rejection of this image of the pulpit star, for it has been too often assumed that the alternative to it is the relegation of the sermon to an insignificant place in the Liturgy and action of the Church. Where the stress has been on liturgical renewal, on the revival of a sense of communal worship, the sermon has often been shunted onto the sidelines as a brief homily on the particular theme of the Church's kalendar or an appeal for the organ fund. Where the emphasis has been on the corporate action of the Church as a catalyst for social change, the sermon has been used as a means for stirring the conscience and goading into action. In neither case have there been great expectations. The sermon has been secularized, withdrawn from the mainstream of worship, and considered as not much more than a commentary of little consequence. Meantime "the hungry sheep look up, and are not fed."

I believe that this disparagement of the sermon has not, on the whole, been shared by the laity. There is a sound instinct in most congregations still which seeks the food of the Word, and expects a sermon really to be a means of grace. It is time for the clergy to recover from this loss of nerve and respond to the demand for preaching that is both biblically nourishing and thoroughly integrated in the life of the Church. That is the real alternative to the prince of the pulpit.

When I speak of the preacher as a churchman, I have in mind, first of all, that he is not a loner spinning ideas out of his personal experiences and interpreting the faith without reference to the communion of saints. He stands there surrounded by the Church Catholic in heaven and on earth and is a spokesman for something much bigger than himself. He is a man under orders. He is ordained to declare, in Word and sacrament, that which was committed to him. This doesn't mean that he is the puppet of

66

the organization, unable to deviate by a hairbreadth from the party line. In the freedom of the Spirit he declares what he really believes, and there is a streak of happy heresy in the great preachers of any age. But he knows that there are limits beyond which he cannot go. He may find himself reveling in new interpretations of familiar passages of the Bible, throwing its imagery around with wild abandon, plunging through its history with an almost irreverent gusto, and making startling applications of its teaching; but he knows that the written Word is his anchor, the authority under which he stands. The churchman will also be aware that he not only speaks *to,* but also speaks *for,* the congregation. An element of preaching is the voicing together of those things we believe. The old "Hallelujah!" and "Amen!" are never far away when the authentic gospel is being declared.

As a churchman the preacher will never detach the sermon from its place in the ordered worship of the sanctuary. He will not be like a cat on hot bricks until the great moment comes for his ascent into the pulpit. He will not make every moment of the Liturgy subservient to the theme of his sermon. He will not fiddle with his notes while the Scripture is being read or an anthem sung. Nor do I think he should make such a distinction between the sacrament of the Word and the sacrament of the bread and wine that when the latter is celebrated his sermon becomes a "meditation." He will endeavor to keep the sermon in its proper place in the rhythm of the service, close to the reading of the Scriptures, and integrally related to the subsequent prayers and dedication.

Just as true preaching cannot be isolated from the ongoing worship of the Church, neither can it be divorced from the role of the pastor. In these days of specialization, there is a danger that the concept of a multiple ministry might be interpreted to mean that one man can devote himself to pastoral work while another is almost exclusively the preacher. I have written before of the young preacher's dream of an ideal setting for the preparation and delivery of a sermon. According to this fantasy, which was presented to me as an eminently desirable arrangement, the preacher would spend his week in a soundproof study without a telephone, well insulated from the noise and distractions of the outside world, lined with the best commentaries, concordances, and works of reference, and with a passage leading directly from it to the pulpit. There the perfect sermon could be produced, and at the close the preacher could speedily reach his haven without the distraction of shaking hands with a single soul. Nothing could better illustrate the difference between a polished production of the homiletic art and real preaching. The sermon constructed in the isolation booth could be theologically immaculate, structurally perfect, thoroughly biblical, beautifully illustrated, logically impeccable—yet a total failure as an instrument for the Word of God. Why? Because it lacks incarnation; it has never been earthed in the experience of the preacher with the people to whom he speaks. The man "sent from God" is not a hermit conceiving his oracles in isolation from the passions, the joys, the sorrows of Tom, Dick, and Harry, and delivering them from his private Sinai. He is sent right

68

into the world to know it at first hand and to be vulnerable to every tremor of his neighbor's pain or joy. That is why the Word of God can be heard in the stumbling words and technically inadequate sermon of a parish minister who really knows and loves his flock, and perhaps not at all in the polished discourse of the cloistered scholar.

The pastor-preacher is a Moses who never gets the children of Israel off his back—and doesn't want to. He's not the impresario who says to his secretary, "Tell that nuisance to go to hell—I'm composing a masterpiece on Christian love." (This does *not* mean that any hypochondriac has instant priority when a preacher is concentrating on a sermon!) He's sent from God to live with people, talk with them, listen to them, feel what they feel, and only after he has been through the dusty streets does he mount the pulpit steps. Like his Lord he must be responsive to that tug on the sleeve when at his busiest. ("You're crazy," said Peter, "all this crowd around you and you ask, Who touched me?") Do any of the recorded sermons of Jesus sound like lucubrations composed in some cave above the Dead Sea? Don't they—parables and all—come right out of his daily shoulder-rubbing with ordinary men and women? The sermons of the apostles in the early Church had this same smell of the earth, and the same warm pastoral care. Paul could fill a book with his masterly exposition of the gospel to the Romans and yet end by sending his love to Priscilla, Aquila, Epaenetus, Mary, Andronicus, Junia. . . . He could preach to the Corinthians the most dazzling sermon ever penned on the Resurrection and go straight on, "Now concerning the collection." He could take the

Philippians soaring into the heavenly places and then ask two bickering ladies to make it up. ("I beseech Euodias, and beseech Syntyche, that they be of the same mind in the Lord.") The entire Bible stands witness to the pastor-preacher as the man "sent from God."

The role of the preacher in relation to his congregation has to be seen in still another light. I am speaking now of the connection between what is said in the pulpit and what goes on in the weekday activities of a living church. It should hardly need saying that there ought to be some relationship between the kind of thing that is being said from the pulpit and the active program of the parish. I don't, for instance, feel flattered if someone remarks to me that he is not at all interested in the reflection of our church's life in the pages of the *Church News* but subscribes for the sake of the printed sermon. If he sees no connection, then there is something wrong with the sermon—or with the activities. This is not to say that a preacher's emphases will always coincide with what some members of the church want to be doing, but a healthy church implies that a marriage has been arranged between the Word in the pulpit and the activities of the congregation, and "what . . . God hath joined together, let not man put asunder."

Let me speak first of the individual response to the Word. Every preacher has heard the question that was asked immediately after the first Christian sermon ever preached. We read that when Peter finished speaking on the day of Pentecost "they were pricked in their heart, and said unto Peter and to the rest of the apostles, Men

70

and brethren, what shall we do?" When that question ceases to be asked, then we are really in trouble, and when the preacher forgets as he composes his sermon that it could indeed be asked, then *he* is in trouble. I think, however, that there have been some misconceptions as to the role of the preacher at this point. The prince of the pulpit has left us a dubious heritage.

There is, for example, the image of the *moral arbiter*. At one time, in both Protestant and Catholic traditions, the clergy were expected to deliver clear maxims to be followed at home, at work, and in public life. Whether or not they were obeyed was another matter. The preacher declared the Christian rules for living, and the church member knew what was expected of him or her. The rules might be detailed and strict, or general and lax, according to the temperament and convictions of the minister, so presumably lay people shopped around a bit rather like the Catholic seeking a compatible confessor. I need hardly tell you that the day is long past when the laity will meekly accept the moral dictates of the pulpit, even though guidance is regularly sought.

When that image disappeared it was replaced in some quarters by an even more damaging conception of the preacher's role. This I call the *vicarious puritan*. In those sections of the Church where a pseudo-puritanical code of behavior concerning such matters as drinking, smoking, gambling, and frivolous entertainments had been accepted, it often happened that the laity quietly dispensed with any such restrictions but insisted that they be represented for them by the man in the pulpit. *They* might throw over the

71

traces, but *he* was still to be in harness, the symbol of a morality they no longer wished to practice. The shadow of the vicarious puritan lay over the whole church edifice, fostering that double standard that still plagues the churches—according to which a Christian is one kind of person within the premises of the church and someone quite different elsewhere. Needless to say, the vicarious puritan is a greater distortion of the preacher's role than most of the priestly concepts that Evangelicals have so violently rejected. It is a total repudiation of the "priesthood of all believers," as well as a device for sheltering from the consequences of unwarranted beliefs. In more sophisticated circles today this concept survives in the notions of the preacher as the one who does the praying for which one claims not to have the time, who expresses the social conscience that is nagging in the background, and who even vaguely does the believing on behalf of the wistful skeptic.

The "man sent from God" in the biblical tradition is neither of these two things. He is certainly not a substitute for the personal obedience of the believer. Nor is he an arbiter of morals. Both of these illusions spring from a legalistic distortion of the Christian way. It is assumed that there is a set pattern for Christian living that can be read out of the Bible and formulated by the preacher, and that there is an answer to moral problems that will be identical for every member of the Church. What we find in the New Testament is, indeed, guidelines by which to measure our response to the gospel in everyday life, but nothing in the way of a moral Baedeker or any uniform image of the complete Christian. And we find the greatest diversity of styles of life among those who are responding to the Word. (Take Peter, James, Paul, and John as striking examples.) The preacher, then, cannot be there to try to impose a moral uniformity, or to give a textbook answer to the question "What shall I do?"

If it does not sound too pretentious I would define his role as that of an *enabler*. If the Word of God really comes to us through the sermon, if Christ is thus really present with us in the mystery of preaching, then we are being enabled to fulfill our calling as Christians in every-day life. Without laying down the law for all matters of morality, the preacher has the duty to expound the ethics of the Bible to which the entire Christian community has given its allegiance: to interpret and illuminate in the light of his knowledge of church history and current theological thinking, and thus to enable a member to make informed decisions on the questions that arise from day to day. To the complaint that a preacher ought to be more specific the answer must be given that, while from time to time he may feel compelled to a "Thus saith the Lord" on some specific issue, he is by no means equipped to sound off on topics about which other members of the Christian community have much greater knowledge than he, but is, in fact, charged by them to give the theological, biblical, and ethical insights for which he was trained.

More important is the enabling that comes from the proclamation of God's grace. The preacher has, above all else, been charged to make known what Paul calls "the unsearchable riches of Christ." Among these riches are the reality of forgiveness, the liberation of the Spirit, and the uniquity of God's love in Christ. These things have to be declared in such a way that the worshiper is truly empowered for Christian living and Christian decision. The preacher is by no means the only enabler in the congregation but has been given the privilege of conveying to the company of believers the light and strength of God's grace. He is not that light; he comes to tell about the light. He is not only sent by God; he is called by his fellow Christians. I make no apology for referring to the fact that the preacher is one to whom, in effect, his congregation has said, "We've made it possible for you to live without selling soap or stocks, driving a bus, or teaching school: in return we expect you to equip yourself to expound the Scriptures and minister to us the fullness of the gospel of Christ." In such simple terms I would define the role of the preacher as the enabler, the minister of the Word of God.

In the same way the preacher should enable a community of Christians to express the gospel together in a common mission to the neighborhood, the nation, and the world. This is something different from his being the leader, the organizer, the agent of every enterprise a church undertakes in the name of Christ. Once we have gotten rid of the notion of the Superman in the pulpit who calls the shots on everything from the flowers in the chancel to the missionary budget, we can release the multiple energies of a Christian congregation. This does not mean that the preacher is the one who declares what the gospel implies in our present situation and then lets others go and do it, but that his primary function is to release the charismatic energies of the whole body of believers by the preaching of the dynamic Word of God. He will enable a congregation to see its mission as a response to the command of Christ, to move beyond the self-interest of a local parish to minister to the needs of the world, to focus on the work of reconciliation, to have the ecumenical outlook of the New Testament to mobilize the immense variety of gifts within the fellowship, and to realize the amazing grace by which alone the true activities of a living Church can be sustained and expanded.

The role of a preacher, then, is neither that of a prince of the pulpit, nor of a moral arbiter, nor of a vicarious puritan, nor of a promoter and jack-of-all-trades. He is the "man sent from God" with a particular gift to offer among the others to be found in any gathering of Christians. We need to recover the full meaning of the Church as a community where a variety of gifts are demonstrated within one fellowship of the Spirit, and thus to integrate preaching again in the total life of a congregation. "There are varieties of gifts," wrote Paul, "but the same Spirit. There are varieties of service, but the same Lord. There are many forms of work, but all of them, in all men, are the work of the same God. In each of us the Spirit is manifested in one particular way, for some useful purpose. One man, through the Spirit, has the gift of wise speech, while another, by the power of the same Spirit, can put the deepest knowledge into words. Another, by the same Spirit, is granted faith; another, by the one Spirit, gifts of healing, and another, miraculous powers; another has the gift of prophecy, and another ability to distinguish true spirits from false; yet another has the gift of ecstatic utterance of different kinds, and another the ability to interpret it. But all these gifts are the work of one and the same Spirit, distributing them separately to each individual at will" (NEB). We might list the gifts differently in our congregations, but who can miss the enormous emphasis on the presence of the Spirit?

I began by caricaturing the prince of the pulpit as a charismatic character of isolated stature. I would end by reminding you that the charisma can be real and true. For "charisma" is a Christian word. It comes from the New Testament and means a gift of the Spirit. The role of the preacher today, as in the past, is to offer this particular charisma in the total fellowship of believers and the service of the world.

5

Evangelism
in an Electronic Age

"All things
to all men...to save some"

When the "man sent from God, whose name was John" preached, he expected something to happen. This was not a commentator on current events with a theological point of view—although he might have sounded like that to any passing journalist from Rome. This was not a rabbi building up a congregation in the faith—otherwise he would have been in the synagogue, not out there in the desert by the Jordan River. This was not a wandering moralist expounding the good life and denouncing the bad. John was a man with a purpose, and his words were designed to produce a radical change in the men and women who heard him. He aimed at conversion, a turning round, a change of mind and heart. He did not look for compliments on his oratory, but for a response to his God. No one could walk away from his sermons saying,

"Old John was in good form today: that's the stuff to give them." He pinned them down with a definite choice. Either they would signify their repentance by going under the waters of Jordan and emerging to a new kind of life—or they would not. This baptism was the sign that something had happened. The Word was alive.

The Prologue to John's Gospel makes it clear that this life-changing Word was to be the theme of the gospel of Jesus. There was to be no automatic response as if the world just waited for someone to say that everyone really believed. Something had to happen. "He was in the world; but the world, though it owed its being to him, did not recognize him. He entered his own realm, and his own would not receive him. But to all who did receive him, to those who have yielded him their allegiance, he gave the right to become children of God" (NEB). The Word of God asked for decision, acceptance, and a new kind of life.

Jesus' own ministry began with a preaching mission. Mark tells us, in his breathless way, that "after John had been arrested, Jesus came into Galilee proclaiming the gospel of God: 'The time has come; the kingdom of God is upon you; repent, and believe the Gospel'" (NEB). We can only try to imagine what the content of this preaching was. Mark goes racing on to tell us how Jesus began to assemble his disciples who were also to announce the Good News. But we surely miss the point if we think of the words of Jesus as merely illustrative of the good life and not as a challenge to believe, to accept, and to follow. The words of Jesus were, of course, backed by the challenge of his life and the signs of his healing and reconciling power, but he had an amazing confidence in the power of the spoken word to convert, to turn ordinary people so completely round that he could talk of their being "born again." When he sent his disciples out he empowered them for two specific tasks: "He sent them to preach the kingdom of God, and to heal the sick." "They departed," we read, "and went through the towns, preaching the gospel, and healing every where." This was no comforting and consoling mission to the religious. It was a direct challenge to the entire population, to each man and woman that they met to accept the gospel of Christ.

If we skip then to the book of the Acts and examine the activities of the infant Church, we shall not be surprised to find that this preaching for a verdict, this life-changing ministry, was the order of the day. The first act of the newborn Church at Pentecost was a sermon, and a sermon that demanded a decision—a decision that, once again, was to be marked by the sign of baptism as an indication that something had really happened, and new life had begun. To put it crudely, Peter looked for converts—and got them: " 'Save yourselves,' he said, 'from this crooked age' " (NEB). Then *those who accepted his word* were baptized, and some three thousand were added to their number that day. The preaching mission was off to a good start.

Think for a moment of the monumental task these simple people had set themselves. They honestly believed that by their own stammering words the life-changing news of the risen Christ would turn the world upside down.

Their little sermons were to be pitted against the vast network of ancestral religions, the deified emperor of Rome, the brilliant philosophers of Greece, and the growing influence of the mystery religions and the occult. Absurd, arrogant, pretentious—the adjectives hurled against Christian evangelism ever since would seem most justified right then. Yet, as we know, within three centuries Christianity became, for better or for worse, the official religion of the Roman Empire.

The word is out—evangelism, preaching designed to convert. I've spun through the records for one reason only —to make plain that the proclamation of a life-changing Word that demands a decision has lain at the heart of the Christian gospel from the very beginning. It is the enduring mystery that through words spoken and heard the story of Jesus comes alive in such a way as to elicit an allegiance to him as Savior and Lord. Thus every preacher who truly gives witness to the Light is bound to be an evangelist, whether he likes the name or not.

Since the word "evangelism" is being tossed around again in the seventies, after a season in the ecclesiastical doghouse, it might be well to examine what it means. There seems little doubt from the New Testament usage that it means this declaration of the gospel through which the Holy Spirit leads men and women to accept Christ as their Lord and to unite with his Church. Some might quarrel with that last phrase on the grounds that church membership is a subsequent, and optional, step on the part of the new believer. If we are thinking about the mechanics of getting one's name on the roll of a particular congregation, this may be so; but there is no question in the New Testament of anyone being an individual believer unattached to the fellowship that is the Body of Christ. In a sense, receiving Christ, confessing him, being baptized, and being incorporated in his Church, are for the first Christians indistinguishable: "Then those who accepted his word were baptized, and . . . added to their number" (NEB).

Why, then, should this activity ever have been relegated to the fringe of the Church's activity, or handed over to the more excitable sects and the stars of the sawdust trail? One reason is simply the success of the first wave of evangelism we have been examining. For the end result of the "Christianizing" of the Roman Empire was the "Christendom" which dominated the thinking of the Church until comparatively recently. The Roman Catholic and the major Protestant churches conceived of a Christian society within which the entire population was at least nominally part of the Church. There was thus no compulsion felt to evangelize anybody except insofar as the baptizing of each successive generation could be considered in that light. Nor, for many centuries, was there much consideration of the duty to bring the gospel to those other parts of the world that lay beyond the frontiers of Christendom. Even that travesty of evangelism known as the Crusades faded away and Christendom settled down to a long period of quiet coexistence with Islam.

It was thus only those who rejected the notion of a Christian nation or Christian continent who concerned themselves with evangelism. The established churches looked sideways at a Wesley, a Whitefield, a Carey, a Moody, and all who were, in their eyes, tainted with "enthusiasm"—which was their word for those who took seriously the possibility of conversion and the demand for decision. This accounts for the suspicion toward evangelists and evangelistic campaigns that still haunts the major denominations—a suspicion that has been augmented by the Elmer Gantry school of revivalism, with its atmosphere of showmanship and peculation.

It is time to awaken from this dreamland in which Christian churches are cosily settled in a Christian land, leaving any evangelistic efforts to the individual enthusiast or the fanatical fringe. There is no Christendom any more. Nor is there any nation on earth that could properly be described as Christian. Our world is not divided into a solid Christian bloc confronting other areas that can be neatly labeled Islamic, Buddhist, Hindu, or animistic. Instead of such vertical lines we have a horizontal line running round the world, where a minority of Christians confront a seething mass of religions and pseudo-religions in every land, including our own. The opponent of evangelism who talks about the folly of trying to export "our religion" to lands which are perfectly happy with their own is living in the distant past. In the first place, the content of evangelism is not "our religion" but a universal gospel we ourselves received from the Middle East. In the second, there are today no communities where the ancestral religion holds undisputed sway. Everything is in flux. And in every nation the Christian Church is meeting the massive opposition of rival faiths and philosophies. It is an illusion

to think that, if the Church were to give up any attempt
to evangelize, everyone would live happily with the faith
of their fathers. For we are living in a period of intense
"evangelism," not only by sects and cults of all kinds, not
only by renewed Moslem and Buddhist faiths, but by
Marxism, nationalisms, and humanisms with every instrument of modern propaganda. If, for instance, the Church
ceased to evangelize in Africa or the Far East, someone
else would be busy on the job. Similarly, the parent who
does not want his children exposed to Christian evangelism
has no guarantee that they will not be swept up by the
Mormons or the devotees of Krishna-consciousness.

The question is not whether evangelism is a legitimate
activity of the Church, or use of the sermon, but how it
should be done in the modern world. If we reject the
techniques of proselytism which imply an arrogant and
unloving attempt to corral others into our particular religious fold, and a lack of respect for another's sincere
convictions, then how do we go about fulfilling the command "Go forth . . . and make all nations my disciples"
(NEB)? In reaction against the narrow soul-winning, head-
counting, scalp-hunting approach, many are now using
the word "evangelism" to mean almost any activity of a
Christian or a church. Just as the word "mission" is now
used to cover a multitude of virtues from being active in
politics to running a day care center, so we are told that a
Christian "evangelizes" every time he opens his mouth, and
a church by simply being there. While it is good to be reminded that the gospel is declared, and the mission of the
Church fulfilled in a thousand different ways, we cannot

83

escape the sharp definition of the New Testament, the passionate call to present the gospel in such a way that the unbeliever will believe, and the skeptic find in Christ "the way, the truth, and the life."

This will not be done without renewed conviction on the part of all church members, and—since I am concentrating on the role of the preacher—a loyalty in the sermon to "those things which are most surely believed among us." Evangelism can only happen when what is being said springs from a profound belief that what the New Testament reports about Jesus Christ is true. This is not to say that the real evangelist is one who blindly accepts all that has been considered orthodox belief in the more conservative sections of the Church, and certainly not that he implies that any prospective Christian has to close his eyes and swallow an immense amount of dogma, miracle, and obscurantism before he can become a disciple. What is wrong with the Fundamentalist is that he fails to distinguish what is indeed fundamental, and loads the Christian gospel with the impedimenta of his tradition. But there are convictions that underlie the confession of Jesus as Lord and Savior that cannot be blurred. There are beliefs about his incarnation, crucifixion, and resurrection that cannot be made palatable by subtraction. There is a grace of God to be experienced that cannot be translated into merely secular terms. The preacher, if he is to be an evangelist, has to be able to say, "This I believe—God help me—and I want you to believe it too." Is it not rather strange that this should be considered presumptuous by many who adopt exactly the same attitude when conveying their ideals to their children or enlisting a friend's enthusiasm for their favorite poet or composer?

There is, after all, a difference between believing and trusting the God we find in Jesus and not having such a belief and trust. That simple proposition ought to deliver us from the thought that somehow the Christian gospel can be reinterpreted and reshaped in such a way as to be acceptable by any reasonable man or woman of goodwill. There is no evidence at all that the Christian preachers and writers who have gone farthest in reducing the content of the faith and adjusting it to what they love to call "the modern mind" have been more successful in winning recruits to Christianity. On the contrary, as C. S. Lewis used to point out, nearly every person we hear of who has been converted to Christianity as a mature man or woman has ended up with a generally orthodox theology and in one of the more traditional doctrinal sections of the Church. There is, indeed, something rather insulting to an agnostic in trying to persuade him that he is really a Christian all the time. He knows better.

To be convinced about the essence of the faith is one thing: to communicate it in this Electronic Age is quite another. There has been an unfortunate tendency in our Protestant churches to confuse loyalty to the historic gospel with adherence to a pattern of behavior or verbal formulae that date from the generation before last. The gospel has been entangled in a forest of taboos, clichés, and sentimentalisms that had their origins in the late nineteenth century in the English-speaking world. (For example, there is the phrase that many consider the touchstone of evangelical truth, "accepting Christ as your *personal* Savior"—an expression nowhere to be found in the Scriptures; and the assumption that a real convert will not drink, smoke, or gamble—matters about which the New Testament is conspicuously silent.) Even in those sections of the Church where this form of piety has disappeared, the gospel is still shrouded in dated language and social conventions that make it hard for the modern pagan to know what is being declared. We have to ask ourselves: Would a sincere and sophisticated young man or woman with absolutely no background of religion really *hear* the gospel in a typical Sunday service, or would it be smothered in our accustomed verbiage and ecclesiastical trimmings?

Here is the first challenge to the man or woman in the pulpit. Recognizing that the pews are not exclusively filled with trained and believing Christians, that there is no longer a homogeneous group of denominational loyalists to be spoken to, and that some may be there out of sheer curiosity, the preacher has to break through with words, phrases, images, and symbols that convey the gospel to the contemporary mood. I am not speaking of that futile attempt to appeal to "the modern mind" (which preachers and theologians are notoriously wildly wrong in diagnosing); nor of the feverish search for the latest jargon or slang (the older preacher is sure to fall into the trap of using the "with it" language of ten years ago—I have just done so). I mean disinfecting our language from churchiness, avoiding the tired professionalism of the pulpit, not using those illustrative stories that no one but a preacher would ever think of telling, and getting out of those rhetorical ruts so deeply carved by our training and experience.

If it is true that this is a visual generation, we may need in the future to combine the use of words with the actual projection of pictures, still or moving, in the course of a sermon, or with the skillful introduction of drama and the dance. The Electronic Age offers possibilities for the imaginative use of visual images that could go far beyond our current conception of "visual aids." But, even without such dedicated contraptions, the modern sermon can appeal to the inward eye with the images that are often so much more powerful than the most polished argument. The preaching of Jesus seldom resembled the structured discourses with which we try to convey his gospel. They consisted more of pictures flashed on the inward eye, or poetic lines to linger in the mind and spark the imagination. The evangelist in the pulpit today must be aware of the power of the picture, the image, the symbol, the gesture, the unexpected interruption, to bring to life the gospel and free the Spirit for his liberating work.

Now we must face the major frustration for the modern preacher-evangelist. The vast majority of the people whom he would like to reach with the gospel of Christ are not there in church at all. There may be some consoling statistics to show that an extraordinarily high percentage of the American public attended church last Sunday (I mean extraordinary compared with any other country or any other century), but here in New York we must be aware that only a tiny fraction of the population is likely to be within a church or synagogue with any regularity—and New York, I reckon, is the shape of things to come. It is here that we have to deal with the question of how to make disciples among those who are almost totally alienated from any religious tradition and for whom the language of the Church is often stranger than Greek. It is here that we have to ponder Paul's confession, "I am made all things to all men, that I might by all means save some."

"All things to all men . . . by all means." It is a strange confession from a man who is commonly regarded as a hard-nosed dogmatist who stuck by his habits and opinions come hell or high water, and he most certainly does not mean that he thinks of himself as a religious chameleon ready to change color according to his environment. He is just saying as emphatically as he can that, for the sake of gaining disciples for Christ, he was willing to meet all kinds of people on their own ground, and was open to new methods of proclaiming the gospel.

When we think of the formidable obstacles to the work of Christian evangelism in the Roman Empire of his day, we can hardly imagine that Paul would have been the least bit daunted by the secularized metropolis of our day. He would, in fact, have been much more at home with our situation than with that of a church-dominated community of a hundred years ago. Without the slightest suggestion of "conforming to this world" he would tackle the work of transforming with all the means this world has to offer.

There is a peculiar challenge to the Church, and therefore to the preacher, in the present situation. It has been customary to say that our problem has been to present a gospel that speaks of the sacred to a thoroughly secularized society, to try to give meaning to the spiritual in a materialist age. On the whole the major churches have tried to meet this situation by an emphasis on the secular, by an insistence that the Incarnation means that the Word became *flesh* and therefore the gospel can only be apprehended through the concrete, physical aspects of our life together. This was a healthy reaction to an unbiblical "spirituality" that regarded evangelism simply as a matter of "saving souls," but it moved rapidly in the direction of eliminating the spiritual altogether. The secular was to be celebrated, salvation was to be seen in terms of social action for the removal of injustices, and worship lost the dimension of transcendence. It was all very well to insist that the Word was made flesh, but soon the concentration on the flesh led to a virtual obliteration of the Word as the revelation of the living God. Instead of the Church penetrating the secular with its word of the sacred, the world penetrated the Church, and evangelism was secularized.

It is ironic that just when the churches were hastening to declare their concern with the secular, to eliminate the note of the supernatural, and to welcome a world "come of age" in which man would assume godlike qualities of control and direction, the so-called secular world dramatically revolted against the assumptions and hopes of materialism, scientism, secularism, and the computerized utopias. We are now addressing with the gospel not so much a post-Christian as a post-secular age. We are not speaking of a Savior and Lord to those who feel the need

89

of neither, but to those who are gasping for a world that is fuller and richer than that disclosed by our instruments, more mysterious than moon shots and supermarkets, and offering some meaning and direction from beyond. Our task, then, is not to persuade people that they need salvation, not to convince them that there might perhaps be something resembling God somewhere around, nor to emasculate the New Testament message by removing all hint of miracle, but to find the way of presenting the story of the crucified and risen Christ so that it takes on new life, unencumbered by the mechanism of our ecclesiastical traditions. This means that the evangelist has to break through the suspicions that attach to the organized churches, and reveal a Christ who offers supremely what is being sought in the cults and theosophies of our new day.

This is a campaign that has to be waged on several fronts at once. There has to be this reawakening of preachers and church members to the centrality of evangelism in the Christian life, so that it is not treated as a specialist department. Then there will have to be a massive effort in the field of what I call pre-evangelism, meaning by that the preparation of the public mind and emotions for the reception of the message of Christ. In military metaphor this is the softening-up of the enemy positions. By that I am referring to the obvious fact that, by and large, modern literature, art, popular entertainment, and the news media are dominated by a purely secular, or at best humanist, point of view. How many novels, plays, or movies express anything that could even remotely be called a Christian attitude to life? When religion appears it is usually in its least attractive aspects, and the evangelist in particular is a favorite subject for caricature. I am not asking for propaganda pieces, or for literature and art that make a specific religious appeal, but for a generation of Christian authors, composers, painters, scriptwriters, and commentators who will consecrate their gifts to capturing the positions so long held by the opponents of the faith. The Church's neglect of the arts, suspicion of the media, and inclination to despise positions of popular influence, have reaped their reward. We have already seen how this generation has responded to a production like *Godspell* or the sound of "Amazing Grace." The hard edges of skepticism and rationalism are already melting. It is time for a skillful, graceful, and penetrating Christian counterattack. We need to remember that in a similar time of confusion and search the early Church not only outlived and outloved the pagan world, but outthought it too. This is pre-evangelism.

For the direct presentation of the gospel to this postsecular world the preacher has at his disposal instruments for which the apostles would have sold their birthrights. Can you imagine Paul with radio, television, and modern electronic equipment within his reach? Everyone knows that the churches have extended their ministry by these means—but how slowly, how clumsily, and how unimaginatively! In the early days of radio the best they could think of was to sling a microphone onto the pulpit and let the listening public overhear what was going on. We have progressed since then, but what denomination has spent even a fraction of the money they should have invested in this miraculous means of reaching into millions of homes with the Christian gospel? How many preachers, including this one, have given anything like enough thought to the ways in which radio and television should be used? By and large, the media have catered to the convinced in the field of religion, and the major churches have made no combined effort to use every available talent to present the unbeliever and the indifferent with the challenge of the gospel.

6

"How Long, O Lord, How Long?"

...And Other Questions Concerning the Conception, Production, and Delivery of the Sermon

In approaching the very concrete question of how a sermon actually comes into being, from the first dawn of a thought in the preacher's mind to the peroration on Sunday morning, I am more than ever aware that no one person can prescribe the rules to be followed. Whenever I read lectures on preaching in which the author spells out the exact steps to be taken in producing a sermon with an air of "This is the way: walk ye in it," I feel like answering, *"Your* way, brother, not mine." He tells me, for example, to have a well-stocked card index of quotations and illustrations. I don't and I won't. Or he says, "Never begin writing until you have a complete outline." I never have. Or he says, "On no account take a full manuscript into the pulpit." I do. Preachers will approach their task with as great a variety of style and habit as doctors, columnists, or conductors of symphony orchestras. A how-to book to be slavishly followed is for the lame and the halt, not the healthy and mature. Any job beyond the most mechanical brings out great differences in personality and approach, and a creative task like preaching demands the fullest expression of the individual, the liberty to be oneself.

It doesn't follow from this that the preacher works in isolation and can learn nothing from the confessions of his brethren. There is no such thing as a completely original preacher who owes nothing to the thoughts, style, habits, and discoveries of others. In this sense there are no completely original poets, dramatists, or composers. Shakespeare, whom we might well consider the towering example of original brilliance of thought and expression, drew freely on the works of his contemporaries, helping himself to their plots, their characters, and their tricks of the trade. If someone were to tell me that a certain preacher is unique and totally original in his thinking, his expression, and his delivery, I should be inclined to say that the only thing original about him is his sin—and that he shares with the rest of us. So there is some value in pinning a man down and saying, "Tell us how *you* go about it."

It also seems only right that one who has spoken freely about the contemporary religious situation, the worship and service of the Church, the place of the sermon in it, and the theological backbone of preaching, should be required to indicate what all this adds up to when he is actually at the business of preparing and delivering a sermon. Need I add that there is also a legitimate curiosity concerning the actual practice of those who preach, just as all of us are curious to know how an artist who has lectured us on the theory of painting actually goes about choosing a subject and mixing his paints. So, although I was tempted in what follows to use an impersonal noun, saying, "The preacher then does thus or so," it occurred to me that it is far less immodest and dogmatic simply to say, "I." For then you know that this is simply one man's way and not a homiletical rulebook.

The gynecological metaphor with which I have approached this topic was deliberately chosen. For a sermon, like any creation of the mind and spirit, involves something of the agonies and joys of the physical creation of new life. When Jesus spoke of his death and resurrection and indicated that the Christian life would be lived under the sign of "joy out of sorrow," he used this same metaphor: "A woman when she is in travail hath sorrow, because her hour is come: but as soon as she is delivered of the child, she remembereth no more the anguish, for joy that a man is born into the world." If there is to be real joy in the creation and delivery of a sermon there is going to be some sorrow and anguish in its preparation. The lack of zest and joy that is to be found in much contemporary preaching may be the result of an avoidance of the agony of preliminary labor of mind and spirit. We delude ourselves when we think that the entire process of creating a sermon should be one long ride along the heights of enthusiasm and spiritual vigor and there is something wrong if we find ourselves staring at a blank piece of paper with the paralyzing feeling that we have really nothing to say or get miserably stuck with an idea for which we cannot find the words. Similarly a congregation deludes itself if it thinks that a sermon which is simply expressed, vividly illumined, and vigorously preached must have flowed effortlessly and joyfully from a well-trained mind and spirit. The enduring mystery of preaching involves the discipline of hard work and the very real pangs of creation. It is hard for some to believe that a preacher alone in his study with his feet on the desk, staring into space, may be doing his hardest work of the week. When I think of the assumption that preaching is, after all, an art that can be easily mastered, and a sermon something that can be put together by a competent practitioner in an odd moment between committee meetings, I am reminded of Alexander Pope's scathing reference to the second-rate poets of his day as "the mob of gentlemen who wrote with ease."

If preaching is held to be in any sense a divine commission, if it is to be a vehicle for nothing less than the Word of God, the genesis of the sermon will surely be in the atmosphere of communion with God that we call prayer. Before one can dare to speak of the Lord in the third person, which is a precarious undertaking for any mere mortal, there must be an encounter with him in the second person, which is ultimately the only solid ground for faith. What I mean is that speaking *about* God is full of pitfalls, and we constantly risk making him seem to be someone we can objectify as one among others, while speaking *to* God is the only way to know him as one infinitely beyond anything we can say about him. So, before I preach, saying "he," I pray, saying "thou." Such prayer, which I cannot claim to be as extensive and intensive as it ought to be, is not simply a request to be given the theme for next Sunday's sermon in one flash of inspiration (such a prayer, in my experience, is rarely answered in those terms!). It is rather a pondering in the conscious presence of God in which all kinds of things, like the needs of the congregation, the national mood, passages and personalities from the Bible, revealing remarks one may have heard, the voice of conscience, a concern for some cause, an illuminating extract from some book or article, or memories of vivid experiences and theological insights from the past, are held in the light of his will and his grace. There may well be a specific "Lord, speak to me that I may speak," but the prayer I am talking about is rather that which surrounds the entire life of the preacher as pastor, prophet, poet, evangelist, enabler—and human being. I might add that even the well-known habit of mind-wandering in prayer can, on occasion, yield an undeserved bonus in the form of a sermon idea that slips into consciousness when one is trying to concentrate on something else.

Let me now come solidly to earth and place myself just a few days before that dread moment when the exigencies of the American printed bulletin demand instant satisfaction. Immediately there come to my mind the admonitions of those who speak of the preparation of sermon topics for a whole season, months ahead, or the solemn example of those heroic brethren who write every sermon for the winter during their summer vacation. In the spirit of "each to his own way" I say, "God bless you; but I am not built

97

that way." I have never written anything worth reading, or spoken with any animation, except under pressure. For me, the deadline does it. But I would quickly add that leaving sermon decisions to a time reasonably near that of delivery is for me a matter of conviction as much as concession to temperament. I want to snuff the atmosphere as I undertake the preaching assignment. I want to sense the contemporary power of the Word. As the pace of our world accelerates it seems to me less and less possible to decide in August what one will preach in November. After all, Karl Barth did not say that the preacher is the man with the Bible in one hand and *last year's* newspaper in the other. For the same reason when I depart to preach in some conveniently distant church and take with me a sermon that has already been preached, I find that not only can I not go very far back into the barrel, but I must reword and relive what I committed to paper weeks before.

Let me speak of a typical Sunday coming up which does not automatically suggest a sermon topic. It's not Christmas, and not Easter, and not Stewardship Sunday or an ordination of elders. There are, of course, the churches and the preachers who are guided by the use of a lectionary every Sunday of the year, and may feel that they have been blessedly spared this agony of what the theme should be. But they too have to decide what the emphasis will be as they expound the assigned text. (And they too may have to come up with a sermon title that is not too like the one of the year before.) For me, the first turning of the mind and spirit to the upcoming sermon normally occurs about the weekend before. The firm decision as to topic, text, readings, and hymns must be made by Tuesday noon.

There are occasions—in my experience comparatively rare—when a text or a topic grabs one by the throat. You *know* that this is what must be preached next Sunday. Normally I find that the decision comes from a wrestling with the two factors that control the preacher's task—the Scriptures and the *kairos*. *Kairos* is that Greek word which the New Testament writers employed to indicate time as actual and decisive (for clock time, the linear succession of events, they used the word *chronos*). *Kairos* is the existential moment, and I am using it here to indicate the preacher's sense of what is happening in the world, in the community, in the Church, in his congregation, right now. Without the Scriptures the preacher will have nothing to say to the *kairos,* except to analyze, to criticize, or to offer some hints as to how we can stuggle along with a certain amount of success and peace of mind. Without the *kairos* the preacher will find himself declaring biblical truths that seem to hang in the air without any attachment to life as his hearers are experiencing it.

In my experience the first thought for the sermon comes either from a passage of Scripture that seems to speak to the *kairos,* or from some pressure of the *kairos* that suggests a search in the Scriptures. In other words, I find myself drawn to a Bible text that has then to be related to our contemporary situation, or led by some current event, some obvious need, some straw in the wind of the Spirit, to seek the Word of God. In the choice of topic, of course, some considerations of balance and common sense play

99

their part. These include such questions as: Have I neglected certain areas of the Scriptures, and certain great themes of the faith? Am I keeping a balance between the doctrinal, the devotional, the ethical, and the "prophetic"? Have I been drawing too much on certain personal experiences, or not enough? What did that chance remark about a sermon suggest? And—never to be forgotten—Am I getting into a rut?

There may, or may not, come a time—say, on Tuesday morning when the Spirit seems to say, "That's it—now, go to work." It may be that one is still hesitating and confused. At this point I remember a warning of one of my professors against what he called "text-hopping." I have learned to know what he meant. And I have learned too that a text and topic chosen with little conviction or enthusiasm may lead to a better sermon than one that seemed to catch fire at first glimpse, and then die away in the throes of composition.

After the theme has been selected and necessary choices made of readings and hymns (and, if your church expects it, a piece for the front of the bulletin—which should be selected for its bearing on the theme, or its stimulus to worship, and not be one of those pious trivialities with which we insult the intelligence of the congregation) what happens next? That depends on the personality and habits of the preacher. For me it is a time of rumination in the course of which I may, or may not, jot an idea down on the back of an envelope. For twenty-four hours or more I make no effort to write the sermon. I think about it, sometimes intensely, sometimes vaguely. It is in my mind as I go to sleep, and when I wake up. It turns around inside me as I walk from home to church, as I sit in a bus, or as I wait for an elevator. (In some New York hospitals a whole sermon can fall into shape before that elevator arrives!) Then there will be the books or articles that come to mind that bear on the subject and, of course, the commentaries. As the time for actual writing approaches I try to do the exegesis of the text, finding out as much as I can about the meaning. I compare various translations. I use a concordance to track down other uses of certain words and phrases. I avoid reading someone else's sermon on the same text or theme (which is what some commentaries are) and concentrate on the Scripture itself. I try to let the Bible speak as if I'd never read the passage before.

Then, having made sure that before I sit down to my typewriter I have a good idea what the first paragraph is going to be, I begin to write. My practice is almost invariably to write about half the sermon on Thursday morning and the other half on Friday morning. At this point the deadline takes over. I have learned to pay no attention to the demon who says, "This isn't the moment; you're feeling heavy, liverish, distracted, uninspired: wait for that blessed moment when you're on top of the world and raring to go." One of Screwtape's colleagues is, I believe, specially delegated to make this suggestion regularly to the preacher—and to most other writers, I suspect. (His other trick, at this point, is to invest all the junk mail on my desk with the utmost allure so that it demands to be studied right away.)

The question that arises now is whether one should write a sermon completely, or work out an outline from which to speak. The arguments are familiar. A written sermon will tend to have a literary form that inhibits free communication. As they used to say, "It will smell of the lamp." Since a sermon is the impact of the Word by the power of the Holy Spirit at the moment of delivery, how can it be prepackaged? A sermon that is written will probably be read, with consequent loss of real contact with the hearer. These considerations are outweighed by two facts that are decisive for me. The first is that only by writing in full do I know that the work of preparation is really done; and the second is that we all have a vastly greater vocabulary at our disposal when we write than when we speak. As one who would much rather preach twenty sermons than write one, I should be tempted to arrive a little too quickly at the conclusion that the work was done; and, although words do not exactly fail me when I am standing on my feet, it is worth the effort to discover better ones for the purpose. Again, the written sermon remains as a record of what has been said, and therefore some kind of a safeguard that it will not be said again in the too near future.

The question of immediacy is an important one. There is certainly no reason why the Holy Spirit should not be in action as powerfully while the sermon is being written as at the moment of delivery. But this means that the writing must be done in full consciousness of the presence of a congregation and with the inner ear attuned to the sound of the spoken word. In other words, the event is already happening as the sermon is being composed. Such an effort of the sanctified imagination will help to limit the occurrence of purple passages that decorate a page but die in the pulpit, or turns of phrase that are literally unspeakable. The art of writing must not be allowed to take over, as it will without constant reference forward to Sunday morning. This is one reason why I very seldom write an entire sermon without a break.

Let me turn now to the use of the Bible in the composition of a sermon. The preacher is not a religious free lance, but stands under the Bible's authority. It is the Word in Scripture that underlies all true preaching. Even if a particular sermon is not expository in the sense of staying close to a section of the Bible, it must be soaked in the biblical atmosphere. And that means something very different from mere citation of texts in support of some thesis of the preacher. The insertion of familiar quotations from Scripture no more makes a sermon biblical than the dragging in of the name of our Lord in the last paragraph makes a religious essay a Christian sermon. True biblical preaching comes from a knowledge of the contents of Scripture and a confidence in its power. Mark tells us of Jesus' reply to the Sadducees, who had produced the silly story about the woman who had had seven husbands, and come up with the question about whose wife she would be at the Resurrection: "You are mistaken, and surely this is the reason: you do not know either the scriptures or the power of God" (NEB). Could that also be his comment on much that passes for preaching today?

What emerges from a sermon is not the hasty exegesis

103

of last week but a lifetime's study of the Bible. And what makes a sermon biblical is not the quantity of Scripture cited but the confidence of the preacher in the power of the Word. It is in the course of composition that this reliance will be in operation. We have surely reached a point where Scripture is regarded neither as a static textbook from which to cull unarguable support for our declarations, nor as a museum piece to which an occasional reference should be made. The Bible is alive in a way that neither current fundamentalism nor old-fashioned liberalism really recognizes. It is through its thorough humanity, as revealed by a critical study of its literary and historical background, that the divine Word burns into us today. The questions that have agitated both literalists and modernists have little to do with this dynamic of the Word. It is not even a question of digging frantically back to discover the precise meaning of the original texts—important though they may be for Christian scholarship. The Bible comes to us in the communion of the Church. Each part is loaded with the devotion of the ages, and illumined by the Spirit as men and women have met their God through these words. With open minds as to the value of this book or that, we can accept the canon of Scripture as a fact of the Church's life. The biblical preacher knows that there is a power here that is part of the enduring mystery, and he has confidence that even the most unlikely texts may come alive in unexpected ways.

The late Harry Emerson Fosdick was a pioneer in what was called the "topical" sermon, which was at the time a refreshing break with the heavy and distant expository style that dominated the pulpit. Yet, as is evident to the discerning eye in all his sermons, he was drenched in the thoughts and language of the Bible. Because he did not sling texts around verbatim many were deceived into classifying him as a nonbiblical preacher. He had the skill to employ the Bible in such a way as to let the Word shine through with a new clarity and power. It is unfortunate that many latched on to his "topical" approach without anything like his knowledge of Scripture, so that a school of preachers arose whose topical sermons were related to Scripture as distantly as a forty-second cousin. The renewal of preaching in our day, if it comes, will spring from knowing the Scriptures and the power of God and not from new-found skills in titillating the topical.

It is only after an effort to master the contents of the Bible that we are free to work at the fascinating task of weaving it into the sermon in such a way that the Word of God can be heard by our contemporaries. There are these endless questions. Is an occasional passing reference enough, or do many today fail to recognize such characters as Noah, Lot's wife, Daniel, the Elder Brother, or the Unjust Steward? What version should we use? Do we paraphrase and retell the story? How do we steer between the Scylla of appearing to be talking about the long, long ago and the Charybdis of a slick and cute modernization? Must we avoid words like "atonement," "justification," or even "grace"? How can we be faithful to the text and yet avoid irritating a congregation with remarks like "Of course, in the original Greek, it doesn't mean this at all"? I am not offering answers to these questions, but suggesting that they are a lot more important than a search for the latest psychological or sociological jargon with which to adorn our sermons, or an eye for quotable quotes.

It is important for me to have from the beginning some idea of where the sermon is going. It has been said that every effective sermon either begins in Manhattan and ends in Jerusalem or begins in Jerusalem and ends in Manhattan. In either case there is movement, and, let us hope, purpose. The real disaster is a sermon that begins nowhere in particular, wanders all over the lot, and ends in the familiar territory of "So what?" The main reason (I have discovered from bitter experience) for slowing down to a crawl or a total standstill when writing a sermon, is not really knowing where one is going or what one really wants to say. While every live sermon will take off in unexpected directions, and thoughts will come that were undreamed-of in the mental preparation, there has to be a discipline that directs and leads to some conclusion. That discipline will also entail the hard labor of moving from the abstract to the concrete, and the translation of the language of the schools into that of the reader of the *New York Times*. The preacher suffers all his life, not from the fact that he was theologically trained, but that so much of his reading, his thinking, and his conversation with his colleagues is conducted in the professional language of theology, or the shorthand of the ecclesiastical world. We tend to be at home with abstractions, and excited by ideas that leave the layman cold. A story is told of a professor of theology who visited an outstation of a Christian mission in Korea, and began his sermon—which had to be translated—something like this: "In our approach to ultimate reality we tend to proceed either inductively or deductively." The translator paused, and then said, "I am here to tell you what Jesus Christ means to me." Unfortunately such a translator is not always available, although one can hope that the Holy Spirit will perform this function when a sermon is flying high. The truth is that it is much easier for most preachers to write fluently in an abstract and technical way than to compose what Wordsworth called "language such as men do use." We do not solve this problem by abandoning the effort to express biblical truth in mature contemporary terms, and presenting platitudes in language such as children do use. It would be my guess that more sermons offend by "talking down" than by talking over the heads of the hearers. Our models here should be, not the slush and slogans of the commercial, but the prose of a first-class journalist, or the language of a first-class poet.

I make no apology for talking here about very practical matters of style, method, and technique. For what we are considering is the *expression* of the Word of God in the language of today. Expression here means incarnation—the Word of God taking on the flesh of our daily speech. Dorothy L. Sayers, in a book called *The Mind of the Maker,* drew a fascinating parallel between the doctrine of the Trinity and the creative process with which she was familiar as a writer. She wrote of God the Father as representing the Idea, the original creative power; of God the Son as the Expression, that idea translated into flesh and blood; and of the Holy Spirit as the Communication, the moment of reception, the point of contact. This inadequate summary of what was something of a *tour de force* rather than a theological thesis might illuminate what is happening at this point in the birth of a sermon. We have thought about the Idea: we shall be soon dealing with the Communication. What happens when a sermon is prepared on paper is the attempt to make the Word visible, audible, concrete. Just as the eternal Word became flesh in Jesus Christ, so the biblical witness to him has to be fleshed out in the language and imagery of today. If we are to hold to a sacramental view of preaching, we shall work at this business of finding the equivalent of real bread and real wine—that is to say, expressions, images, symbols, that are in current use, that have some resonance to the modern ear. Laziness at this point will result in language that is neither biblical nor that of everyday, but a tired echo of the piety of fifty years ago, or the polysyllabic platitudes of ecclesiastical committees.

Let us suppose, then, that the sermon is on paper. The idea has been expressed. The biblical passage has been brought into contact with an actual situation. The sermon will have been read over, and perhaps some changes made. What then? I have to confess that I have no real temptation to tinker and revise, but prefer to put it right out of my mind for twenty-four hours: not with any sense of verbal inspiration, or to say with Pilate, "What I have written I have written," but simply in the belief that little good will come from the naggings of perfectionism. The realization that the sermon has not yet come to birth keeps me from any sense of a *fait accompli,* of being locked in by what has been prepared. Anything may happen between midday on Friday, when I normally finish, and Sunday morning—in recent memory, for instance, the assassinations of President Kennedy and Martin Luther King. At the back of one's mind must be the thought that this product of many hours' labor may have to be drastically revised, or even, to extend our gynecological metaphor, aborted. (I have to confess also that, on the occasions when my manuscript has mysteriously disappeared during the hymn before the sermon, I have had to decide whether to go and search for it rapidly in the robing room or whether perhaps God was telling me something.)

On Saturday night I read through the sermon, silently or aloud. This is the point at which the literary touches may have to be blue-penciled, the need for expansion indicated by an arrow, or some questionable assertions eliminated. I find it is also a time for striking out pseudo-modest redundancies like "perhaps," "it seems to me," "in my opinion," and for getting rid of those bogus characters "the man in the street," "the man in the pew," and "the average citizen." At this point it is more than ever necessary to envision the moment of delivery, to see the sermon as a whole, and to let it speak first to oneself. I do not try to memorize verbally, but to be so familiar with the outline that I could run it over in my mind.

On Sunday morning comes the last read-through, and perhaps a mental re-creation of the sermon during a good walk to the church. A sermon conceived in prayer will, of course, be held in prayer, and delivered with a silent or spoken invocation. But, as I have indicated before, this concern with the sermon should not preclude a real participation in worship. Rather is this the moment to see the sermon as one part of the rhythm of Christian worship which will dictate the mood, the manner, and even the tone of voice in which one begins to speak.

To use the trinitarian analogy again, we are now at the stage of communicating—the peculiar territory of the Holy Spirit. The preacher needs to experience something of the freedom of the Spirit. In human terms, the sermon must now come alive. No matter how much toil and sweat has gone into the preparation, it must now be spoken with direct contact and immediacy. That means an actual rethinking in the presence of a congregation of what was laboriously worked over on paper. There must be no impression of the secondhand, of repetition of something which has already been done. This rules out straight reading, whether from a manuscript or from some point in the back of a memorizer's mind. Like an actor, the preacher has to be sensitive to his audience, knowing instinctively when they are following or when he has lost them, when they are alert and when they are tired, and he must be ready to change pace, repeat, or pause, according to the mood. Unlike an actor, he knows that he and the congregation are engaged together in the common worship of God and response to his Word. I may add that, while rejecting the image of the performer or pulpit star, I believe that we preachers have much to learn from the immense devotion and meticulous preparation of our friends in the theatrical world.

Need I add that everything we have thought about in

the preparation of the sermon, the laboring to conceive, the expression in writing, the energy of communication, will add up to zero if nobody can hear what is said? If that comment sounds too banal to be included in a series of lectures like this, let me retort that, in my experience, the battle has often been lost for want of this particular nail in the horse's shoe. Another text to pin up inside the pulpit for every preacher, from the youngest to the most mature, might be "How shall we hear without a preacher —who can project his voice?"

One last word—about that voice. We have the voices that God gave us, but with the help of kindly friends and the right kind of wife, we can be preserved from the curious inflections and syrupy intonations that are instantly recognizable as a religious noise. I can never understand why when we twiddle the knobs of a radio on a Sunday we are liable to know at once when we are listening to someone delivering a sermon. Must the Good News be announced in a totally different voice than the daily news of the bulletins?

From "In the beginning was the Word" to the sound of the preacher's voice—the journey has taken us through territory which needs to be traveled again in this generation. In my opinion (delete) it is not the sermon that is obsolete, but many of the methods of those who still believe in it, and all the theories of those who have written it off. For the Word of God is alive in Jesus Christ; the biblical record is alive through the Holy Spirit; and there will still be men and women "sent from God" who are

111

called to declare that Word in the living accents of today and tomorrow. In closing I salute them in the belief that among them will be found those whose loyalty to the Word and sensitivity to this new age will engender a fresh and imaginative era of the enduring mystery of preaching.